P9-CAU-787

SOUL
COACHING®

Also by Denise Linn

✡ ✡ ✡

All of the above are available at your local bookstore. The ones with asterisks may also be ordered by visiting: Hay House USA: www.hayhouse.com®
Hay House Australia: www.hayhouse.com.au
Hay House UK: www.hayhouse.co.uk
Hay House Publishers India: www.hayhouse.co.in

SOUL COACHING®

28 Days to Discover Your Authentic Self

Denise Linn

HAY HOUSE, INC.

Carlsbad, California • New York City
London • Sydney • New Delhi

Copyright © 2003 by Denise Linn

Published in the United States by: Hay House, Inc.: www.hayhouse.com
Published in Australia by: Hay House Australia Pty. Ltd.: www.hayhouse.com.au
Published in the United Kingdom by: Hay House UK, Ltd.: www.hayhouse.co.uk
Published in India by: Hay House Publishers India: www.hayhouse.co.in

Editorial supervision: Jill Kramer • *Design:* Amy Gingery

All rights reserved. No part of this book may be reproduced by any mechanical, photographic, or electronic process, or in the form of a phonographic recording; nor may it be stored in a retrieval system, transmitted, or otherwise be copied for public or private use—other than for "fair use" as brief quotations embodied in articles and reviews without prior written permission of the publisher.

The author of this book does not dispense medical advice or prescribe the use of any technique as a form of treatment for physical or medical problems without the advice of a physician, either directly or indirectly. The intent of the author is only to offer information of a general nature to help you in your quest for emotional and spiritual well-being. In the event you use any of the information in this book for yourself, the author and the publisher assume no responsibility for your actions.

Soul Coaching® is a registered trademark.

Library of Congress Cataloging-in-Publication Data

Linn, Denise.
  Soul coaching : 28 days to discovering your authentic self / Denise Linn.
    p. cm.
Includes bibliographical references.
  ISBN 1-4019-0231-6
  1. Self-actualization (Psychology)—Problems, exercises, etc. 2. Spiritual life—Problems, exercises, etc. I. Title.
  BF637S4 L565 2003
  158.1—dc21

                              2003012608

Tradepaper ISBN: 978-1-4019-3071-4
Digital ISBN: 978-1-4019-3021-9

30 29 28 27 26 25 24 23 22 21
1st printing, October 2003

Printed in the United States of America

This book is dedicated to my husband,
David, and my daughter, Meadow.
Their continued support and love
replenish my soul.

Contents

CHAPTER ONE:
Air Week—Clearing Your Mental Self 19

CHAPTER TWO:
Water Week—Clearing Your Emotional Self .. 73

Preface

I remember so clearly the moment I got it—when I finally began to listen to the messages from my soul.

When I woke up that morning, I did not feel any different than I normally do. I shuffled out of the bedroom, stumbled into the bathroom, and squinted at my disheveled appearance in the mirror. Yet as I gazed through my blurry eyes at my image in the mirror and splashed water on my face, fragments of the previous night's dream floated before my eyes. Something about this particular dream struck a chord buried deep inside me. Suddenly it was as if an immense dam broke within me, and I felt something inside shout, *"Enough!"*

It was just one word, but it felt like a thunderbolt rolling through me. I started to sob. I did not really know why I was crying, but I knew that something was wrong with my life. My professional and family lives were good, but sometimes, when I was alone, a quiet desperation would creep over me. I felt like something was missing from my life. It was as if I were waiting for "happily ever after" to begin and my real life to start. And I had been waiting for a very long time.

When I was in high school, I thought that when I finally moved away from the violence and sexual abuse at home, my "happily-ever-after life" would begin. But when I moved out, nothing seemed to really change. Then I was sure that my perfect life would finally start after I got out of college . . . when that did not work, I decided that happiness, security, and contentment would start when I got married. As you can guess, that did not happen either.

There was always some future goal that I had to fulfill before my real life began, such as owning a home, having a baby, writing a book, or traveling. All the time, I kept waiting for "happily ever after," but there was always some obstacle in the way or something I had to accomplish first. I thought that when I was done with my "to do" list, then I could relax and do what I wanted, but somehow I never did. Consequently, I was never really content, and I always postponed my heart's desire.

But on the morning when I heard *"Enough!"* I got a message straight from my soul. I knew it was time to stop waiting and awaken to the fact that I *was* living my real life. I needed to realize that life is never perfect and "happily ever after" isn't something that happens in the future—it is an inner state of being that must begin inside me.

My soul spoke clearly to me that morning. It was time to slow down the frantic pace of my life and begin to listen to it. It was time to stop living my life in accordance with the expectations of others and giving to everyone else without giving to myself. It was time to love, accept, and cherish myself, and take a deep breath and know that the Creator was by my side.

Out of the realizations that were initiated that morning came Soul Coaching, a program that can help you listen to the heartfelt messages from your soul. If you are reading this book, then perhaps the time is right to begin your journey into the realm of your soul.

There is no better time to start than right now, because if not now, when? Your life will always be filled with challenges, but you do not need to wait for everything to be perfect. You need only believe that you are on the right path, and you *are* on the right path—from a spiritual perspective, we all are. In fact, we always have been, *even when we did not know it.*

I believe that every experience that we have had, whether we judge it as bad or good, has been a vital part of our spiritual path. Every aspect of life is important and valuable. Every experience is essential for our growth as a spiritual being. The more I realize this, the more I understand that there is no "way" to happiness— happiness *is* the way. It is a journey, not a destination. However, there are often blockages to knowing this. This 28-day program will help you clear them.

When you stop waiting until you lose ten pounds, you finish your degree, you find a new job, you get married or divorced, the kids leave home, you win the lottery, you retire, or you achieve self-confidence and self-esteem, then you can finally start to live a life that is truly fulfilling and authentic.

If you feel that you have to completely heal yourself before you can live your authentic life, you will never reach your dreams. However, if you accept yourself and know that within you is a place that is sacred, loving, and whole, then slowly your darkness will be replaced with light—because there is nothing that cannot be redeemed when it is washed with the sanctity of love and acceptance.

When you initiate your grand adventure into the realm of the soul and begin to clear the inner debris from the deepest place within you, slowly but surely, stress and struggle begin to disappear—your life was not meant to be a struggle. Softly and gently, you will find that love, inner peace, and joy begin to radiate from you out to others and the universe.

This is the essence of Soul Coaching.

Acknowledgments

My deepest gratitude goes to Marika Burton. She inspired me to enter into the field of Soul Coaching, and for this I am eternally grateful.

I am also immensely thankful to the wonderful individuals (and especially the "Raindancers") who have gone through my Soul Coaching program. Their insights about the transformations that occurred for them motivated me to present this program to you.

To LuAnn Cibik, your grace, support, and love have been remarkable. Thank you so much.

To Pattie Hanmer, you are one of the true gifts in my life. I am honored to know you.

To Allison Harter, I am incredibly grateful to you for "Playing Full Out!" I don't know what I would have done without you!

———✠———

What Is Soul Coaching?

Do you know who you are and why you are here? Do you know what your mission in life is? Are you aware of the daily guidance from your soul? No matter how great your outward success is, if you do not know the answers to these questions, you might feel that something is missing in your life. That is where Soul Coaching comes in.

Soul Coaching is a powerful program that anyone can do. It is a process that takes you to your spiritual source and helps you find meaning and sacredness in your everyday life. It allows you to take an honest look at yourself and your life, face fear, release old negative patterns, get motivated, and step boldly and joyfully into your future.

Once you have committed yourself to the program, life will seem to unfold in a remarkable, almost magical, way. Declare that you are ready to discover your authentic self and are willing to dedicate one month of your life to doing it, and loving forces in the universe will coalesce to propel you in the direction of your destiny. Synchronistic events and seeming "coincidences" will begin to expand exponentially in your life.

I am not quite sure why this happens, but once you commit to this program, it is as if the universe has heard your declaration and amazing events seem to emerge within your life, all aimed at a deep soul cleansing and clearing. The events of your life are not accidents. If you have this book in your hand, it is probably the right time for your soul detoxification.

The aim of Soul Coaching is to align your inner spiritual life with your outer life. It helps you clear away mental and emotional clutter so you can hear the messages from within. It also helps you discover your purpose so you can design a life that supports that purpose.

Regular life coaching usually focuses on the attainment of a goal or a dream, which differs from therapy, as the intention there is usually focused on emotional healing. Soul Coaching is different from these modalities, as its primary aim is to clear away your inner debris in order to connect you with the wisdom of your soul.

The understanding of who you are can never be told by another. It is only when *you* reach into the wellspring of your being that the truth of the soul springs forth. Just remember: *The soul loves the truth.*

This 28-day program is about telling the truth to yourself about your life. When you do this, your energy increases; when you do not, you become depleted. Many people are exhausted and burnt out because they are not being starkly honest with themselves. When you are authentic, your soul thrives.

Telling the truth to yourself is not the same as telling it to others. In other words, if you pass a mere acquaintance on the sidewalk and they ask, "How are you?" even if you have just had a fight with your husband, found out your child is on drugs, and are coming down with a cold, it is still okay to reply, "I am fine, how are you?" But if you tell *yourself* that everything is fine when deep inside you know that it is not, your soul suffers.

What Is the Soul?

Soul is a word we use to describe the central or integral part of something, or its vital core. In its most profound sense, the word also describes the essence of every human being—it is that place within each of us that is infinite, eternal, and universal.

The soul is a source that gives rise to form, yet it is unknowable. It is elusive by its very nature, yet it must be nurtured and cared for. We can intuitively understand what its needs are, yet never fathom its depths. It is the substance that links our body and spirit to the greater forces of the universe.

The closest that I have come to directly experiencing my soul was as a result of a near-death experience at age 17, which was caused by a random act of violence.

I had gone out for a ride on my motorbike in the country-side of the small farming community where I lived, unaware that a stranger was following me in his car. Once we reached an isolated spot, he purposely rammed his car into my bike, and the force of his attack threw me to the ground. This man, who had killed several other women in similar attacks, then got out of his car and shot me.

I was left for dead on the side of the road. A farmer found me, and I was taken to a nearby hospital. I remember so clearly what happened as I lay in the emergency room: The tremendous pain that I was experiencing abruptly subsided, and everything became very quiet. I felt myself lifting out of my body and entering into a dark sphere that seemed to softly cocoon me. I don't know how long I was there, but suddenly a bright light penetrated the darkness, and I found myself in a realm of exquisite golden light. It was so peaceful. I experienced a deep awareness of belonging, inner serenity, and sublime connection to the essence of my soul. I felt that I was home, and I never wanted to leave. But a calm, resonant voice told me that I could not remain there because my time on Earth was not complete. I was pulled back into my body.

Even though I had sustained eventual substantial damage—including the loss of my spleen, one of my kidneys, and an adrenal gland—in addition to a plastic tube replacing my aorta and a bullet hole in my spine—my memory of that beautiful dwelling place beyond this life still lingers within me.

After this turning point, much of my life was focused on recapturing that sacred space within myself. I traveled to many countries and studied the traditions of many other cultures, but in the end I realized that the answers were inside of me . . . as they always had been. I had been so busy seeking the answers outside of myself that I had not really stopped to look inside. As I began to discover the answers inside me, I wanted to help others on that same journey. Soul Coaching is the process that I created to assist others in finding their sacred and holy inner place.

What Is the Soul Coaching Program?

Soul Coaching is a spiritual journey that is divided into four one-week periods. Each week is dedicated to one of the four elements—Air, Water, Fire, and Earth—for I believe that our memories, beliefs, and emotions are tied in some mysterious and organic way to the elements of nature. By activating these elements within us, we can also activate quadrants of our souls.

For many years I worked as a practitioner using a system I developed that was based on these four elements. I taught this modality to therapists to incorporate into their practices. The system was based on the idea that the elements have an effect on the psyche. I found that when clients immersed themselves in images of the elements, each element evoked different emotional responses, as well as different kinds of memories. The remarkable thing about this elemental approach to therapy is the way that it reveals the emotional impact that the elements have on us.

A proverb from India states that each of us is a house with four rooms—mental, emotional, physical, and spiritual—but unless we go into every room every day, we are not complete. The elements are powerful tools for entering these inner rooms.

Throughout history, the elements have been associated with natural balance and wholeness. Ancient people knew that within each element were patterns of energy that permeated the universe. They used this understanding to develop cosmological models to create a sense of harmony in their lives.

From Native Americans to ancient Greeks, Egyptians, Mayans, Aztecs, Persians, Celts, and Hindus, the mysterious panorama of nature has been divided into separate parts that are designated by the four elements. Egyptian sages fervently believed that reflecting upon the four elements provided a profound understanding of life.

In the mystery schools of Mesopotamia, initiates underwent rigorous rites of Air, Water, Fire, and Earth to test particular aspects of their natures. Hippocrates, honored as the father of medicine, declared that a patient's health depended upon a balance of the four elements. And the great Sufi poet, Rumi, wrote that the four elements were the foundation of life and had a profound effect on the human sprit.

For all of these peoples, the symbolism of the four elements knitted separate pieces of reality into a cohesive whole. Each one brought a gift that gave balance to life. The Spirit of Air gave the wind with its cooling breezes in the summer; the Spirit of Water brought refreshing rains; the Spirit of Fire gave warmth from the sun; and the Spirit of Earth brought forth the hills, mountains, trees, and plants on our planet. The underlying energy of all the elements was the Creator, the Source of all life.

Nature is a melding of the elements—a vast cauldron of Air, Water, Fire, and Earth, and none can exist without the other. Yet, using the individual elements to represent conditions of life can allow for a powerful integration to occur in your life. I believe that when you embark on this spiritual cleansing program, it is immensely valuable to do it in the context of the cycles of nature, as its energy can help bring you home to your spiritual roots.

An Overview of the 28-Day Soul-Coaching Program

- *Days 1–7* are devoted to the properties of Air and are associated with clearing mental debris.

- *Days 8–14* are devoted to the properties of Water and are associated with your connecting to your emotional self.

- *Days 15–21* are devoted to the properties of Fire and are associated with clearing the shadows from your spiritual self.

- *Days 22–28* are devoted to the properties of Earth and are associated with strengthening your physical self.

Additionally, after you have undergone the 28 days, you are encouraged to embark on an inward journey much like a vision quest, which can take from a few hours to a few days. After all the clearing you have done, this will be a time of stillness for the soul to reveal its sacred messages to you.

How Can I Fit the Program into My Busy Life?

No matter how busy you are or how hectic your life is, you can do this program. There are assignments each day, which are divided into three levels. You choose the level at which to participate.

1. Level 1, which is called "Committed to Change!" usually only requires 15 to 30 minutes a day.

2. Level 2, which is called "Going for It!" (and includes doing the Level 1 exercises), will usually take 30 to 60 minutes a day.

3. Level 3, which is called "Playing Full Out!" (and includes doing the Level 1 and Level 2 exercises), takes as long as it takes.

There are some days when you may just participate at the "Committed to Change!" level, and there may be days when you want to "Play Full Out!" You may want to select a level of participation for the entire 28-day process, or you may decide to vary the levels as you see fit.

For example, Day 3 focuses on the clutter in your home and what it means to you. (When your outer life is in disarray, it's difficult to find the stillness to connect with your inner life.) Level 1 suggests that you clear clutter out of one small area in the bedroom or bathroom, such as one drawer or one shelf; Level 2 suggests that you clear the clutter in a larger area of your bedroom, bathroom, or bedroom closet area; and Level 3 suggests that you *completely* clear the clutter from one of those rooms. You may want to choose Level 3, but you might have to wait for the weekend to complete this larger task.

When Should I Start This Program?

Because the program is organized into 28 days, you may choose to start the first day of the month or follow the 28-day moon cycle, starting with either the full or new moon. You might also want to start at the winter or summer solstice or begin in early spring, which is naturally a time of new beginnings. Alternatively, you may want to schedule yourself to do this program during your vacation, or start on January 1. The most important thing is that you begin. Often when you wait until the perfect time, opportunity will pass you by. When you plunge in, even if it doesn't seem to be perfect timing, dramatic results are often produced. Keep this thought in mind:

> *Whatever you can do, or dream you can do, begin it.*
> *Boldness has genius, power, and magic in it. Begin it now.*
> — Johann Wolfgang von Goethe

There are many ways to participate in this process. Since the 28 days are divided into four elemental cycles, you can also do this over a four-month period, or even extend it over the course of a year, assigning one elemental cycle to each season. However, it is often easy to lose your steam if you take a long time to do this program—that is why I have designed it to be completed in 28 days.

Be Gentle with Yourself When You Do This Program

When most of us were growing up, we were taught to judge ourselves harshly if we did not do things perfectly. Well, fear not—you do not have to be perfect for this program to work miracles in your life. Do the best you can, and forgive yourself when you do not do every exercise exactly as described. Almost everyone who has done the program has mentioned that even on the days that they missed or did not fully do the exercises, there was an amazing synchronicity that still occurred for them.

It is important to remind yourself that the goal of this program is personal growth, not just completing assignments. In other words, focus on your accomplishments, not on what you did not complete. *Trust that changes are occurring at a deep level.*

If you have ever tried to unravel the knots in a gnarled ball of yarn, you will remember that the more you struggled with the knots, the worse they got. But if you gently pulled the string around each knot, they unraveled easily.

So be patient with yourself. Celebrate what you did complete, and forgive yourself for what you did not. This is not a competition, it is an unweaving of the inauthentic self and a discovery of your soul.

Everything That Happens During Your 28 Days Is Part of the Process . . . Even If It Does Not Seem Like It

The universe is whispering to you at every moment. There are messages for you in the morning breezes, and there is wisdom for you in the caw of the crow outside your window and in the cadence of an afternoon rainstorm. Even ordinary events in your life carry communications from your soul; however, your mind is often too full to hear it. When you make the commitment to embark on a journey to hear these messages, you will begin to "hear" these messages loud and clear.

Over and over again, people doing this program remarked on the astonishing synchronicity that happened for them. There were mundane coincidences, such as plumbing problems during the Water Week and electrical surges during the Fire Week, but they also experienced more profound coincidences, such as hearing from an estranged family member during the section on relationship healing or receiving an anonymous bouquet of flowers during the section on gratitude. Just know that literally *everything* that happens during your 28 days is part of the process, even if it does not seem like it at the time.

Goethe talked about this phenomenon when he said, "The moment one definitely commits oneself, then Providence moves too. All sorts of things occur to help one that would never otherwise have occurred. A whole stream of events issues from the decision, raising in one's favor all manner of unseen incidents and meetings and material assistance, which no man could have dreamed would have come his way."

There may be times when you notice some resistance to doing the work. That is okay—even this is part of the process. Once you observe it, ask yourself, "Where is this resistance coming from?" This may be the lesson for you for that day. For example, if you feel overwhelmed and unable to complete an assignment, it may just be that your schedule is very full. Or it may mean that you have subconsciously overscheduled yourself so that you do not have to confront the current issues in your life. Pay attention to the issues that arise during the program, and also notice during which element they occur.

Soul Coaching: Alone or with Others?

You may choose to do this program on your own, but you may also decide to do it with others. I have found that it is often easier to complete the program if you have a group of people sharing the experience with you. The support of others can be extremely helpful and motivating.

You may want to gather a group of friends together for mutual support. I suggest that you meet once a week for four weeks to compare your progress and to support each other. You could also meet once a week for 28 weeks, dedicating one week per assignment.

Another idea is to form an online support group so that you update and support each other on a daily basis. You can also log on to **www.Soul-Coaching.com** or **www.DeniseLinn.com** to locate a certified Soul Coach in your area for support and guidance either online or in person. In fact, when I wrote this book, I was also coaching a group of people through the Soul Coaching program via e-mail. Every day I sent a daily message with the introduction to that day's exercises. The feedback about these messages was so encouraging that I decided to include them in this book. You might imagine that through these words, you and I are in communication, supporting each other in our spiritual journeys.

Getting Started

Where intention goes, energy flows. It is important that you take time to get clear on why you are embarking on this 28-day odyssey. What end results do you desire from having participated in this soul journey? What is your intention? Are you really ready to make a change in your life?

Taking time to clarify your intention before you start this program will help determine the form that it takes. Enjoy the 28 days—remember to be gentle with yourself, and cherish your accomplishments. Feel free to do this program in any way that works for you and your life. Your journey toward connecting with your soul has begun. Don't wait for the perfect time . . . the perfect time is *now*.

Listen to Your Soul

First, set aside a few moments of quiet in the morning and evening just to ask your soul if there is anything you need to know or anything that your soul would like to communicate with you. This specific act of intent can open your ability to listen and be receptive to receiving further messages.

Keep a Journal

I suggest keeping two journals during the program. I call the first one your "Process Journal." It is for mental and emotional clearing and can also be used to express your feelings and to write the insights you incurred as a result of the daily assignments. I suggest that you use a three-ring notebook and make or purchase colored tabs, one for each day, which will help you refer back to sections from previous days.

The second journal is what I call a "Joy Journal." Here you might include writing, collages, drawing, poetry, photos—one a day to chronicle the great moments of your day—or anything else that illustrates the joyful or magical moments of each day of the program. No matter what happened on a particular day, there are always special, meaningful, or magical moments—chronicle them in a way that is creative, invigorating, beautiful, or fun.

Daily Affirmations

Every day you will be given a carefully chosen affirmation that is appropriate to the assignment for the day. Affirmations work because what you focus on is often what you create for yourself.

Some people write the affirmations on Post-It Notes and place them on their computer, mirror, or refrigerator as periodic reminders during the day. Alternatively, you can repeat the affirmation to yourself (silently or out loud) throughout the day.

Your word is your wand. If you constantly tell yourself, "I am not good enough," your subconscious mind begins to believe it, and you end up acting not good enough. Consequently, people treat you in a demeaning way. If you feel that most people can't be trusted, you will find yourself surrounded by untrustworthy people. However, if you think that the world is filled with love, you will find love pouring into your life.

Affirmations are usually stated in a positive way, so you may wonder why there are times in this book when an affirmation has a "not" or a "no" in it. I have found that there are rare occasions when using such negative words in an affirmation can actually have more power than a positive affirmation does. Here is an example.

For most of my life I have struggled with feeling overwhelmed. It was a recurring pattern that kept me in a perpetual state of stress. So in order to overcome this negative pattern, I began to use the positive affirmation: *I have too much time and need more to do!* This was great and really seemed to work for me. I felt less overwhelmed.

There would be times, though, when I would occasionally still find myself feeling overwhelmed. It was only when I yelled over and over, "I will *never* indulge in the stupid negative pattern of 'overwhelm' ever again!" that something snapped. Since that time, I have been busier than ever, yet I have not felt overwhelmed. To me, this is a miracle: A so-called negative affirmation worked. (However, if putting a "no" or "not" or "never" in an affirmation does not work for you, change the words so that they *do* work.)

Make a Sacred Contract

I suggest that you create and sign a contract for yourself that clearly states your intention for the next 28 days. It's usually much easier for us to keep our word with someone else instead of ourselves. We are often meticulous in keeping our word to others, yet will easily break a commitment to ourselves. However, *the vows we make to ourselves are even more important to the soul than the vows we make to others.*

If someone continually broke his or her word with you, after a while you would think that that person was untrustworthy. When you break your word with *yourself*, it is a message to your subconscious mind that you are not a trustworthy person and often your self-esteem suffers.

You can make your contract as specific or as general as you like. Use words that work for you and create an honest, realistic contract that you can keep. Here is an example: *"I, Denise Linn, do hereby declare to myself and my Creator that I will dedicate the next month to connecting with my soul. I will endeavor to be honest with myself and others to uncover the truth about who I am. Additionally, during this month, I vow to take time every day to relax and eat according to my nutritional needs rather than my emotional needs. I accept that adhering to this contract attests to the strength of my character."*

Write your sacred contract out on paper, sign it, and date it. You might even want to post it in your home or put it at the beginning of your Process Journal.

Create an Altar

In ancient times, almost every home had an altar, for it represented the intersection between Heaven and Earth. It was a place for quiet reflection and devotion. There is great value in re-creating this ancient tradition while you do the 28-day Soul Coaching program.

An altar does not need to be religious. It can be a highly personal representation of what is most important to you—your hopes and dreams and what you hold sacred. It can be a place to still your thoughts and open your heart to your own intuition. Even if you don't spend time in meditation at your altar, simply having one in your home is a powerful subliminal reminder of that which is sacred.

It is easy to make an altar. All you need is a table or shelf. Spread a beautiful cloth on the surface and then place things on it that represent your intention for your "soul full" journey for the next 28 days. It should only include objects that are true representations of what is in your heart. Additionally, as a suggestion, place objects or photos on your altar that represent each of the four elements and also something that represents your spiritual source.

You are now ready to begin the journey
to the center of your soul.

CHAPTER ONE

Air Week—Clearing Your Mental Self

My Cherokee grandparents owned a ranch in Oklahoma, and I used to love to visit it in the summertime. I spent hours down by the stream that meandered through a meadow on their land, loving the thick warm mud on the bank as it squished through my toes. It was exhilarating to try to find crawfish as they scurried through the rocks, and sometimes I would lie on my back on the grassy bank of the stream and watch the clouds float overhead. It was in those moments that I felt deeply connected to my soul and to the soul of the earth. When I breathed in, I felt like I was inhaling the sun, sky, earth, stream, clouds . . . everything.

That memory reminds me of what you will be doing during this first week of your program. The initial week of the journey to your soul is aimed at clearing mental cobwebs so that you can recapture the sense of wonder and exhilaration that a child experiences lazing on a riverbank watching the clouds roll by, or flying a kite in a summer breeze.

The Air element is often associated with mental activity, organization, commitment, assessment, judgments, rules, and beliefs—or the aspect of your personality that has the capacity to discern, analyze, evaluate, and judge. So this first week is a time to take an assessment of your life; clear out personal, environmental, and business clutter; discern your commitments; and begin to understand your inner rules and beliefs.

The first seven days are devoted to clearing as many unresolved issues as possible that block the mental aspect of self. Do not be concerned if mental challenges come your way this week—instead, use them as an opportunity to clear old blockages. This is also the time to be aware of the air around and within you; it is the time to embrace and be aware of the air, sky, and oxygen around you; and it is the time to breathe in deeply and fully.

The Next Seven Days

For the next seven days when you first wake up in the morning, focus on the air around you. Take a deep breath and be aware of the physical air that surrounds you. Concentrate on the air as it enters your lungs as you imagine inhaling self-acceptance and exhaling self-judgment. By doing this, you will be activating the Spirit of Air that dwells within and around you. As Dr. Andrew Weil once said, "If I had to limit my advice on healthier living to just one tip, it would be simply to learn how to breathe correctly."

During the Air Week, I suggest that you read poetry and inspirational books and quotes to support your mental process. Listen to soothing music, and go on a "media cleanse" to keep your mind clear of blaring advertisements and negative news. Walk every day, and watch the clouds and the trees dance and bend in the wind. Breathe deeply and fully for long periods of time.

During Air Week

- Assess and evaluate your life.

- Clear out your clutter (if you do not love or use it, get rid of it).

- Make commitments that empower you.

- Do things you have been putting off or make a plan for doing them.

- Organize papers/answer letters/make postponed calls.

- Pay bills or make a planned schedule to pay bills.

- Organize your home and office space.

- Examine your core beliefs.

- Breathe/become aware of the quality of the air you breathe.

- Notice the sounds in your environment/ listen to inspiring music.

- Sing/shout/use your voice.

- Communicate your truth.

‡ ‡ ‡

Day I

Hi!

Today is the beginning of a great and grand adventure! You are truly one decision away from a new beginning. If you have gotten this far, you are probably ready for a future that is more meaningful and authentic.

The future is created by the choices that you make today. Making a decision to change does not need to be monumental and earthshaking—it can simply be an inner declaration that you are going to become more aware of the sacred places within you. And as surely as the sun rises, if you make the decision to change your life, the forces of the universe will unite to propel you in that direction.

When you finally garner the courage to make the decision to change, the aftermath is not always easy. Those around you may be threatened by your changes, as stepping into new strengths can sometimes make others feel inadequate. There may even be times when you doubt yourself and feel afraid. However, being courageous doesn't mean that you are not doubtful or afraid at times. It means that you experience those emotions, and then you do it anyway.

Today's exercises are probably the most time-consuming of all the exercises for the month. It gets easier after today. Do what you can, and enjoy the process. (You can come back to the exercises later if you do not complete them today.) This is not a contest or competition. Also, notice any emotions or old memories from the past that come up for you as you do today's exercises.

All my love,
Denise

❧ ❧ ❧

You don't have to see the whole staircase, just take the first step.
— Dr. Martin Luther King, Jr.

❧ ❧ ❧

Day 1 (Air): Life Assessment

The journey to discover your authentic self starts with stark honesty about where you are. Be honest in your self-appraisal.

Affirmation for the Day

"My evaluation of myself is not who I am."
(Continually affirm this throughout the day.)

Today

Priodically take deep breaths, visualizing life-force energy filling your lungs and your body.

Overview

- *Committed to Change!*
  Level 1: Assessing Your Life

- *Going for It!*
  Level 2: Steps and Leaps—Bridging the Breach

- *Playing Full Out!*
  **Level 3: Assessing Your Physical
  Environment and Life Questions**

Level 1: Assessing Your Life

Take some time to assess where you are in your life right now, and write down these thoughts in your Process Journal. Include where you are regarding your health, relationships, finances, career, creativity, and spiritual fulfillment, and write out your intention for the next 28 days.

Level 2: Steps and Leaps—Bridging the Breach

Review the following exercises. Then, in your Process Journal, record the steps or leaps it would take to bridge the breach in each area of your life. There are no right or wrong answers.

Steps and Leaps

This exercise helps you discover the distance between where you are now and where you would like to be. *Your soul loves the truth.* When there is a gap between where you are and where you want to be, this creates incongruity and sometimes even a feeling of inauthenticity.

"Steps and Leaps" is an exercise to help you discover the breach, or distance, between where you are now and where you want to be. For example, if you desire incredible vitality, yet every morning you drag yourself out of bed, drink three cups of coffee before you even get to work, and then spend your entire day in front of a computer, it might be a "huge leap" between where you are and where you want to be regarding your health. On the other hand, if you *are* satisfied with your health, but feel as if you would like to be more consistent in your exercise program, it is just a "small step" to bridge that gap.

Be aware that you are the person who is deciding what the distance of the breach is. If you notice consistent "huge leaps" in your self-assessment, you may be the kind of person who is very self-critical. *Where* you are in your life is less important than the *judgments* you make about where you are. Of course, there is always room for improvement in life, but inner peace comes from accepting and loving where you are now. The first step toward inner healing is *not* to judge yourself for judging yourself.

Ask yourself the following questions for each item below: *Where am I? Where would I like to be?* Be as truthful as you can, and grade the distance in either steps or leaps—such as one step, two steps, one leap, or a huge leap. Notice the areas of your life where the rift is the greatest.

- Self-esteem
- Putting the needs of others before my needs
- Worry/frustration
- Resentment/ bitterness
- Shame/guilt
- Anger/irritation

- Fear (of failure/ success/intimacy/ commitment/ taking risks, and so on)

- Being busy and overwhelmed

- Self-motivation

- Creativity

- Joy/enthusiasm

- Inner peace/ contentment/ fulfillment

- Relationships with friends

- Relationship with lover(s)

- Relationships with family members

- Relationship with the Creator

- Forgiving myself and others

- Sexuality

- My past

- Job/work/career

- Finances/ abundance

- Physical health

Level 3: Assessing Your Physical Environment and Life Questions

The way you organize your outer, physical environment will often reflect (and can even dictate) your inner life. So please answer *yes* or *no* to the following questions, and be honest and rigorous in your assessment.

<u>My Home</u>

I. **Bedroom**

____ I feel safe, protected, and nourished in my bedroom.

____ My bedroom is a haven for my soul.

____ My dreams are insightful and provide a passage-way to my inner realms.

____ The clothes in my closet reflect who I am and who I desire to become.

____ I truly relax and feel safe in my bedroom.

____ I sleep well in my bedroom, and when I wake up in the morning, I am refreshed.

____ All of the objects (paintings, statues, photos, and so forth) in my bedroom give me joy and contribute to my feeling balanced.

2. Kitchen

____ I feel energized, healthy, and vital in my kitchen.

____ Food prepared in my kitchen looks and feels healthy and empowering.

____ My soul feels nourished in my kitchen.

____ I feel creative and get inspired when I prepare food.

3. Bathroom

____ The energy in my bathroom feels cleansing and healing.

____ The bathroom is a place where I purify and renew myself.

____ I feel comfortable and safe in my bathroom.

____ When I look in the mirror, I feel good about what I see.

4. **Living room (family room)**

   ___ My living room is a safe haven for me.

   ___ I love or use all of the objects in this room.

   ___ Friends and family feel great when they are here.

   ___ My living room is clutter free.

   ___ It feels warm and inviting.

   ___ My energy goes up with every object in this room. (In other words, there are no objects in my home that have negative associations. There are also no objects that I dislike but keep just in case the person who gave it to me comes over.)

5. **Dining room**

   ___ When I eat, it is a pleasant, sensual experience.

   ___ I cherish and support my body by eating food that empowers my body and spirit.

6. **Garage/basement/attic**

   ___ I use and/or love the objects that I have stored.

   ___ The objects that I have stored are used periodically. (For example, there are no items such as equipment, appliances, or machinery that are broken or haven't been used in the last three years.)

7. **General home**

____ It feels good to approach my front entrance.

____ The entrance into my home is easily accessible, and I use my front door.

____ Every time I enter my home, I feel welcomed and my energy rises.

____ My home is clean and cared for. (Windows are clean, floors and carpets are vacuumed, closets and drawers are organized, countertops and tables are clear, and furnishings are in good repair.)

____ My plants and animals are healthy and cared for.

____ I love my home and feel great just being in it.

____ There are beautiful things in my home that make me feel good.

____ My home feels healthy and vibrant.

____ There are very few things that I am "putting up with" in my home environment.

____ The photographs of people in my home are of people whom I love and cherish and who love and cherish me.

Answer this question: If my home were an exterior representation of aspects of me and my life, what would it say about me?

My Automobile

____ I love the environment of my vehicle and feel good when I am there.

____ I play radio stations/tapes/CDs that uplift, inspire, or inform me.

____ I feel protected in my vehicle.

____ I care for my vehicle though periodic maintenance, cleaning, and oil changes.

My Work

____ I love my work.

____ I feel creative and inspired when I am at work.

____ I really enjoy the other people with whom I work.

____ I am not "putting up with" any person or any work situation.

____ I feel no undue pressure, and I have the time I need to feel productive and joyous.

____ My place of employment is healthy for my body and soul.

____ I am constantly growing and learning new things.

____ I feel appreciated and supported by my boss, co-workers, and/or employees.

<u>Life Questions</u>

In addition to answering the questions above, write down the answers to the questions below in your Process Journal if you are "Playing Full Out!"

- Where am I now in my life: mentally, emotionally physically, and spiritually?

- What does the purpose of my life seem to be?

- What would I like my purpose to be?

- What am I passionate about?

- What gives me immense joy?

- What is my spiritual source?

- Is my life consistent or in alignment with my values?

- How do other people see me? How do I see myself?

- What qualities would I use to describe who I am now?

- What qualities describe the person I would like to be?

- What have I been putting off doing?

- What do I need to forgive myself/ forgive others for?

- What do I want to do with the remainder of my life?

- What is really important to me?

- What are my goals?

- I have been blessed with skills/gifts. What are they?

- Am I using these skills?

People who fail to make changes in their life usually get stopped by frustration, which is then followed by procrastination. When you feel frustrated, see this as an opportunity to strengthen your soul. Breathe deeply, take a risk, and vigorously plunge ahead. You'll find clarity on the other side—this is the moment for a breakthrough.

‡ ‡ ‡

Day 2

Hi!

Congratulations—you have made it to Day 2! The first couple of days of a new program are usually the most difficult, but you have made it this far. This shows that you have made a commitment to yourself and your personal growth.

Often "commitment" is considered to be associated with another person, but I believe that true commitment is to yourself—it is giving your word to yourself and <u>keeping</u> it. When you are committed to your soul's path, you learn to say "no" in loving ways to others so that you can say "yes" to yourself. This is because you cannot truly help others until you help yourself. The commitments that you make today will create an energy that will expand exponentially throughout your life. You have my support on your journey to the soul.

All my love,
Denise

P.S. As a suggestion, you might want to consider doing this process with a friend or going online to **www. Soul-Coaching.com** or **www.DeniseLinn.com** to find support. Also, remember that participating at Level 2 includes the exercises from Level 1, and Level 3 includes the exercises in both Levels 1 and 2.

Day 2 (Air): Making a Commitment to Change Your Life

After you have begun to assess your life, the next step is to make a commitment to take action. There is power in commitment. The instant that you make a decision to change your life, you have put forces in play that almost magically begin to transform your life.

Affirmation for the Day

"I honor my commitments to myself and to others."

Today

Become even more aware of the air around you: the way it feels on your face, the way a leaf slowly floats through the breeze, the way the clouds drift on the currents, and the way you feel when you inhale and exhale.

Overview

- *Committed to Change!*
  Level I: Commit to Take One Empowering Action Daily

- *Going for It!*
  Level 2: What Are Your Values in Life?

- *Playing Full Out!*
  **Level 3: What Have You Been
  Putting Off?**

Level 1: Commit to Take One Empowering Action Daily

Commit to make an empowering change in at least one area of your life. I suggest that you write it down and post it where you can see it every day as a reminder, as commitment is a day-by-day process. Each day, renew your commitment (and forgive yourself if you did not keep it the day before), as every day is a new beginning. Under-standing the true power of commitment can totally transform your life.

To make a commitment is to take a stand in life—the moment you *are* your commitment rather than it just being something you said, you can actually impact the world.

If there were one empowering thing that you could do today (and every day for the next 27 days), what would it be? Choose one thing, and make a covenant with yourself to keep your word. *Your word is law in your universe.* Give your word to yourself with integrity, focus, and certainty, and with the same intensity that you would use if you were giving your word to the Creator.

Below are some examples of things you can commit to do on a daily basis for the next 27 days. Or you can choose something else not on the list that you know would empower you. What you choose is less important than your willingness to make a commitment to yourself and to follow through *no matter what*.

Examples of daily commitments:

- Dancing with wild abandon for ten minutes

- Meditating for 15 minutes

- Doing yoga for 20 minutes

- Praying for peace

- Taking a walk

- Painting or drawing for 30 minutes

- Doing breathing exercises for five minutes

- Taking a candelit bath

- Cleaning out the attic for 15 minutes

- Working in the garden

- Exercising aerobically for 15 minutes

- Clutter-clearing for 30 minutes

- Sitting quietly doing nothing for ten minutes

- Becoming conscious of what food and drink you have consumed by writing it down

- Drinking six glasses of water

- Lying on the earth and imagining sinking into her soul

Alternatively, you can commit to *not* doing something on a daily basis. For example, you could:

- Limit television watching to one hour

- Cut back to two cigarettes

- Omit doughnuts or fried food from your diet

- Limit your use of profanity

- Stop eating after one serving

Level 2: What Are Your Values in Life?

Your values are your identity. Your sense of "self" emerges from your personal values—in fact, your entire life revolves around them, so it is very important to discover what they are. In this exercise, remember that there are no right values, only the values that are right for you.

Write down your values on pieces of paper and then arrange and rearrange them in different orders until the order of your personal values feels right.

Ask yourself if your life is consistent with your values. If not, make a commitment to change your life, or change your values so that they are in harmony. For example, if your top personal value is "peace and relaxation" but you love day-trading in the stock market and snowboarding, this can create incongruity within you. Consider changing your top value to "adventure" or changing your activities to be consistent with your top value of "peace and relaxation."

Make an inner commitment to live in harmony with your values. When your life is in alignment with your values, deep satisfaction expands within you. (As you proceed with this 28-day program, it is not unusual to find the order of your values changing.)

Examples of personal values:

Love	Passion	Creativity
Peace	Enthusiasm	Commitment to career
Loyalty	Adventure	
Happiness	Intelligence	Courage
Security	Connection to family	Wisdom
Knowledge		Abundance
Joy	Integrity	Determination
	Graciousness	

Level 3: What Have You Been Putting Off?

What have you wanted to do but have been avoiding, procrastinating, or delaying? Make a list of what you have been putting off and then *take action today* on at least one item! (In addition, make a feasible plan to take every one of these items to completion in the future.)

Make a commitment to keep your word with yourself. Share your commitment with a friend or create consequences for yourself (such as what you will buy yourself if you keep your commitment)—you know what it takes for you to keep your word. Do whatever it takes to keep the commitments that you are making this day. The willingness to make a covenant with yourself and then keep it is the first step to true inner mastery.

❖ ❖ ❖

Day 3

Hi!

Today's assignments are about clutter. The power of clutter-clearing cannot be overrated. Maybe you are not exactly clear about what form you want your life to take, but if you start clearing clutter, your authentic self will begin to emerge. It is one of the fastest ways to lighten the soul.

Sometimes it works like magic. For today's assignment, my client Jessica decided to clear her sock drawer. She had a huge tangle of single socks that she had saved over the years, but she said that she hated to throw them away—so she wore mismatched pairs around the house when no one could see them.

Although Jessica's goal was to have a loving romantic relationship, all of her previous relationships had been "mismatched." As she looked at all the "singles" in her drawer, she decided that perfectly matched pairs of socks were a better metaphor for a great relationship, so she got rid of 40 singles and only put perfectly matched socks in her drawer. Jessica said that it was a wonderful coincidence that the next man she dated was such a great "match."

All my love,
Denise

Day 3 (Air): Clearing Clutter in Your Bedroom/Bathroom

For some people it is unrealistic to think that all the clutter in their life could be cleared out in a week (or a month, or even a year). However, even a small amount of clutter-clearing can have remarkable results. When you begin to clear out any clutter in the environment around you, it can have a powerful corresponding effect on the mental clutter *inside* you.

Today, start with your bedroom, bathroom, or bedroom closet. These are the personal areas of the home that often relate to personal areas of your life. Your home is often a metaphor for your life, and the bedroom is thought to be a metaphor for your inner life. The bedroom is also where you spend the greatest amount of time. It is where you dream, rejuvenate, and have intimate relationships, so there are often powerful metaphors within the bedroom that relate to your inner experience of self.

When you are deciding where to start your clutter-clearing, remember your self-assessments from the first day. If you have difficulty letting go of old relationships, then clutter-clearing the things that represent those relationships can have a powerful effect on that pattern.

For example, if you store your old Christmas cards in your bedroom, purge the ones from people with whom you no longer feel connected. And organize the cards from the people you love. Also realize that you can keep the *love* from the people who sent you those cards, but you can throw the cards away.

In your clutter-clearing, celebrate what you <u>did</u> do rather than what did not get done. Also, take each task to completion. For example, it's better to completely clean out one drawer than only get halfway through a closet.

<u>Affirmation for the Day</u>

"There is clarity within me and around me."

<u>Today</u>

Breathe in self-acceptance, and breathe out self-judgment while doing this cleansing yogic breath:

Breathe in for three, hold for three, and exhale for three. (Repeat three times.)

Breathe in for six, hold for six, and exhale for six. (Repeat three times.)

<u>Overview</u>

- *Committed to Change!*
  Level 1: Clutter-Clear One Small Area

- *Going for It!*
  Level 2: Clutter-Clear One Larger Area

- *Playing Full Out!*
  Level 3: Completely Clutter-Clear One Room

Level 1: Clutter-Clear One Small Area

Choose one small area within your bedroom, bathroom, or bedroom closet, such as a drawer or shelf. Clear and clean it thoroughly, and while you do, affirm, *"I am clearing all that I do not need out of my life."*

Notice emotions, thoughts, and memories from the past that occur while you do this. Be aware of the meaning that you give those items and why you have chosen to keep them. Remember this motto: "Use it, love it, or get rid of it."

Level 2: Clutter-Clear One Larger Area

Choose a larger area in your bedroom/bathroom/closet to clutter-clear. For example, clear *all* of the bathroom drawers. Periodically affirm *out loud* with intention as you do this: *"I am clearing all that I do not need out of my life."*

Words have power, and when you say affirmations at the same time that you clear out an area in your home, this speaks powerfully to the subconscious mind. Create an affirmation that matches what you are clearing. For example, if you are clearing out old clothes, you might affirm: *"The clothes I keep magnify my beauty, grace, and joy!"* or *"These clothes are the old me, and I am now releasing the old me."*

Level 3: Completely Clutter-Clear One Room

Choose either the bedroom, bathroom, or bedroom closet, and completely clear it. With every item, ask yourself: "Do I love this? Do I use this? Or have I used it in the last two years?" If the answer is no, get rid of it. Affirm out loud with passion, using your body—for example, punch the air over your head with your fist while proclaiming: *"I am clearing all that I do not need out of my life!"*

Additionally, once you have cleared the clutter, create a space that feels great. Put out flowers, clean the mirrors, or put up artwork that inspires you. Create beauty. If you are working in your bathroom, although the items on the countertops might be necessary, perhaps there is a way that they can be presented in a more attractive way. Is it necessary to have all the lotions, razors, toothbrushes, makeup, prescriptions, supplements, mouthwashes, *and* your hair dryer spread across the countertop, or is there a more harmonious way to store or arrange them? For example, maybe your vitamins could be put into a beautiful jar or basket.

Your bedroom, bathroom, or bedroom closet can be a place of refuge and renewal. It is in these places that you can refresh, revitalize, and nurture yourself. Today, create beauty and harmony in one of these rooms.

When you are complete, light a candle and sit quietly, saying a blessing for the energy in that room to support vitality, peace, and love.

Day 4

Hi!

Well, you made it to Day 4. By this time you should be noticing old stuff/patterns/recurring blockages coming to the surface. Remember: It is just like cream coming to the surface to be skimmed off—it is just stuff, and it is just releasing.

You do not need to necessarily do anything about an issue if it comes up . . . just notice and observe it. This is the energy of Air. To understand this aspect, imagine an eagle soaring overhead as he observes life below from his detached point of view. In other words, become the Sacred Observer this week. And today is a day of self-awareness.

All my love,
Denise

Day 4 (Air): Where Are You Now in Your Life?

We all have thoughts about ourselves, some of which create rigid rules and core beliefs about life. In some cases, our thoughts and inner beliefs are empowering, but in many cases, we have unwise thoughts about who we are and what we believe.

Even though the way we perceive ourselves might not always be glowing, we are each doing the best we can. We did not consciously choose our identity—it was molded by the circumstances of our life and by things that our family and other people told us.

Our identities are shaped by the emotional environment of our early childhood years, which we tend to re-create in adult years. We are programmed by the thoughts and belief systems of our parents, who were shaped by the beliefs of *their* parents. Sometimes we will even treat ourselves the way our parents treated us.

In your quest to connect with your soul, remember that *you are not your identity.* Who you truly are is so much more magnificent, remarkable, and eternal.

To begin to loosen your attachment to your identity, it is important to first become aware of it. Do not try to get rid of it—instead, become the Sacred Observer and examine your ego, self-concept, beliefs, and rules about life without judgment. Observing yourself with a gentle sense of humor will help you find your authentic self.

Affirmation for the Day

*"I love and accept who I am . . .
and who I am is enough."*

> ## Today
>
> *Observe your life while you hold the thought that the events of your life today are neither good nor bad—they are just the events of the day. They are only good or bad depending upon the meaning that you give them.*

Overview

- *Committed to Change!*
  Level 1: Be the Sacred Observer

- *Go for It!*
  Level 2: Your Faults Can Be Your Virtues

- *Playing Full Out!*
  Level 3: Observing Your Core Beliefs

Level 1: Be the Sacred Observer

Your identity is a detailed concept about yourself that you cart around with you through life. It is a jumble of evaluations, opinions, rules, and perceptions about yourself that serves as a filter through which you view every experience. For example, if your filter contains the thoughts and beliefs that this is an angry world, you will continually see angry people and situations around you.

The problem is that you may not be aware of even a small percentage of the enormous number of beliefs about yourself and the world that you hold. Your beliefs about life and yourself are so ever-present that you often do not even know that they are there. They can be likened to the air that is all around us, but we are rarely aware of it. In other words, the more aware you become of the thoughts, concepts, and perceptions you have about who you are, the more you can begin to discern who you really are.

Today, observe your thoughts and the situations around you—become the Sacred Observer. Watch your internal dialogue, and observe the language and words that you use. If you discern that your language is filled with disempowering words, consider substituting more empowering ones. You feel different when you use different words. Changing your language can change your life. For example:

- "I am depressed" can become "I am a little down."

- "I am exhausted" can become "I am recharging."

- "I am pissed off" can become "I am a tad cranky."

- "I am lonely" can become "I am open for love."

- "I am overwhelmed/overloaded" can become "I am stretching myself to discover my capabilities."

- "I have too much to do" can become "I am expanding my horizons" or "I'm seeing what I'm capable of."

- "I am okay" can become "I am great!"

- "I am all right" can become "I am superb!"

- "I am good" can become "I am excellent!"

Be aware of your reactions to the experiences you have on this day. Ask yourself, "For me to feel this way about this situation, what would I have to think and believe about myself and the world?" and write down those thoughts.

Become a silent witness for a day. Without judgment or evaluation, watch yourself, your actions, and your *re*actions. Observe the language you use. Do you use empowering or disempowering language when talking about yourself or about life? Notice the types of thoughts that you think on a consistent basis. Do your thoughts bring you closer to your authentic self or take you away from your source? Write down your observations in your Process Journal.

Level 2: Your Faults Can Be Your Virtues

As you begin to become aware of the perceptions that you have about yourself, you may notice yourself labeling those thoughts as "good" or "bad." The truth is that when you begin to accept the things you do not like about yourself, they can become your assets. For example, instead of condemning yourself for being stubborn, think of "stubborn" as being "overamplified determination." This is a wonderful quality that can be called upon when you need to complete a project or get through a challenging time. The thought then changes from "I am stubborn" to "I am strong and determined."

Make a list of your so-called faults. Next to each one, list how it can be viewed in a positive manner if it were toned down. For example:

- "Flighty" toned down becomes "spontaneous."

- "Penny-pinching" toned down becomes "thrifty."

- "Resentment" toned down is a "strong sense of justice."

- "Perfectionism" toned down becomes a "commitment to excellence."

- "Procrastination" toned down becomes "divine timing."

- "Bluntness" toned down becomes "honest self-expression."

Level 3: Observing Your Core Beliefs

A core belief is a notion that you have held so long and repeated so often that it has become entrenched into your subconscious mind. These beliefs are like a hum in the background that you don't know is there until it stops.

List the positive and negative core beliefs that you have about yourself. After writing your list, think back to when you first adopted that belief, and write that down.

Examples of negative core beliefs:

- Life is a struggle.

- No pain, no gain.

- I need to look after people.

- Nobody can do the job as well as I can.

- I have to do it myself if I want it done right.

- Men/women in my life always treat me badly.

- I am too old to think about a new career.

- I have to fight to get ahead.

- I never finish what I start.

Examples of positive core beliefs:

- I have incredible determination.

- I am always loved and lovable.

- People really enjoy being around me.

- I always complete what I start.

- I succeed at whatever I attempt to accomplish.

- No matter what challenge I encounter,
  I always find a way to overcome it.

- The more I give, the more I receive.

- My life is guided in the right direction.

- All of my needs are met.

‡ ‡ ‡

Day 5

Hi!

This morning such sweet bird songs awakened me. I stretched, hurried outside to greet the day, and took a few deep breaths of fresh morning air. Overhead, the breeze swept through the pines, creating soft murmuring sounds. I felt so embraced by the Spirit of Air.

Today is dedicated to more clutter-clearing! To me, clutter-clearing is modern-day alchemy. It can transform your life.

All my love,
Denise

Day 5 (Air): Clutter—Energy Up/ Energy Down

The Spirit of Air relates to the mental aspect of yourself, and it also relates to organization, clarity, focus, and being able to see afar. To understand this spirit, imagine that you are on a mountaintop. The air is fresh and sparkling, and when you take a deep breath, your entire body feels invigorated. As you look down to the valleys and to the distant sea, it seems that you can see forever.

Clearing out unused or unloved possessions in your home can have this same invigorating effect on your spirit—it can truly be a transformational experience. Your clutter may be draining and depleting your energy. In other words, if the things in your home are not used or do not inspire you or bring you joy, then getting out from under the burden of them can be a soul-fulfilling experience.

There is a good reason why so many spiritual teachings discourage accumulation. A powerful connection exists between the organization of your material belongings and the cultivation of your spiritual growth. It is easy to feel overwhelmed by possessions and lose sight of the presence of the Divine.

When you clear out the "stuff" that lowers your energy, your home becomes a sanctuary. A home that matches the contours of your soul subconsciously affirms that you are completely all right exactly the way you are. It is a place where you explore who you are and what you might become. A soulful home gives you a deep sense of belonging; it is a place on the planet where you can sink your roots and feel safe—a home for the soul.

I don't expect that you can clear out your entire house/office/car in a few hours (or even a few weeks or months), but even taking a few steps today can begin a process that can have a huge impact on your life. Remember that clutter to one person is not clutter to another. If it brings your energy down, it is clutter; if you love it or use it, it is not. Releasing clutter can open the space for a new vitality to surge into your life. You are on a spiritual journey, and clearing clutter helps your home becomes a refuge for your soul.

Affirmation for the Day

"Fresh, invigorating energy fills my life."

Today

(If possible, do this exercise outside.) Close your eyes and connect with the Spirit of Air. Feel the air around you, where it touches your face and body. Imagine that you are aware of the air within you. Air is not only in your lungs, it is in every one of your cells, oxygenating and cleansing them. Then take deep, slow breaths, imagining that you are filling your body—and your life— with sparkling, invigorating vitality.

Overview

- *Committed to Change!*
  Level 1: Energy Up/ Energy Down

- *Go for It Level!*
  Level 2: Clutter Questionnaire and Clearing One Area

- *Playing Full Out!*
  Level 3: Employ the Power of Metaphor

Level 1: Energy Up/Energy Down

Every object in your home will bring your energy up, take it down, or be neutral, even if you are not consciously aware of it. For example, my client Susan once bought a vase right after she had an argument with her husband. Even though she liked the vase, every time she looked at it she subconsciously associated it with the argument, so it subliminally lowered her energy. Yet Susan wasn't even aware of this fact until she did the "Energy Up/Energy Down" exercise.

This exercise can be done in two ways. You can choose one or the other, or both.

First method: Close your eyes, relax, and imagine that you are walking around your home. See yourself picking up different objects and opening different drawers. Notice where your energy seems to go up, and where it goes down—in other words, is there a certain room or particular object that really lifts you up or makes you feel depressed? Later, you might want to consider getting rid of the objects that bring your energy down and displaying the ones that bring it up.

Second method: Actually walk around your home, staying in touch with your feelings and your body sensations. Notice where your energy seems to wane and where you feel revitalized. Touch different objects, and notice what happens to your energy. After doing this exercise, you may want to make adjustments in your home.

Level 2: Clutter Questionnaire and Clearing One Area

Because objects are invested with symbolism, clearing things out of your home can have a direct effect on your psyche: Sooner or later you will experience the positive consequences of clearing the debris out of your home. For this exercise, answer this clutter questionnaire and then choose one area to clear (it does not have to be big).

When clutter-clearing, it is valuable to be aware of the "I am my house" syndrome. When you do not want someone to visit because your house is messy, or when someone drops by unexpectedly and you profusely apologize for the mess, you are identifying with your home. There is nothing wrong with being proud of your house—however, from a spiritual perspective, you are not your home. You have things, and they influence you, but they are not who you are. When you are clearing out clutter, notice how much of your identity is attached to the objects in your home.

Answer *yes* or *no* to the statements below:

I. **Bedroom**

_____ I wear the clothes in my closet. In other words, I do not have stacks of clothes that I never wear because:

- they do not fit but might someday,
- I paid a lot for them,
- they might come back in style,
- they were a special gift.

____ I feel satisfied with the organization of my bedroom and bedroom closet.

____ The space beneath my bed is clear.

2. Bathroom

____ I only keep medications in my medicine cabinet that are not past their expiration date.

____ The items in my medicine cabinet have been used in the last year (such as perfume, shaving cream, and so forth).

____ My bathroom cupboards and the areas beneath the sink are clutter free.

3. Kitchen

____ The appliances (toaster, refrigerator, coffeemaker, and so on) are in good repair.

____ My kitchen counters, cupboards, and floors are clean.

____ The food in the cupboards is less than a year old.

4. General Home

____ My home is in good repair (no cracked windows, faulty plumbing, leaking roof, and so on).

_____ I am able to find things easily without a long search.

_____ I do not have piles of newspapers and magazines that I have not read.

_____ I do not have spare parts to things that are unknown to me.

_____ I do not have stacks of broken things that I have been meaning to fix.

_____ I only buy things that I need (and not what I already have but have forgotten about).

_____ I complete the projects I start. (In other words, there aren't a lot of unfinished or never-started projects lying around.)

5. Vehicle

_____ My vehicle is in good repair.

_____ I change the oil regularly.

_____ I periodically rotate the tires and have a tune-up.

_____ My car is clutter free.

6. Desk/Office

_____ My desktop is organized and clear.

_____ My papers are neat and filed.

_____ Piles of papers on my desk stay no longer than two weeks.

_____ My bills are paid, and/or I have a plan to pay them.

___ I am debt free.

___ I spend my money wisely.

___ I am up-to-date with my taxes and/or have a plan to pay them.

___ My computer files are only the ones I need and use (in other words, there is not a lot of computer clutter).

___ I de-clutter my files periodically.

Reviewing your answers should give you a clear sense of those areas that need some clutter-clearing. It is valuable to make positive affirmations as you do this. For example, if you decide to clutter-clear your car, you might affirm: *"I travel forward in my life easily and effortlessly!"* Get the feeling that you are able to move forward with more ease and grace.

Level 3: Employ the Power of Metaphor

Choose one additional area from the above list and clear it out. Continue to ask yourself: "If this represented something about me and my life, what would it be?" Employ the power of metaphor with your clearing. For example, if you have financial difficulties, you might consider going through old bills and financial papers, affirming: *"I am clearing away blockages, and abundance is flowing into me!"*

Keeping clutter because you might need it someday is a negative affirmation. It tells your subconscious mind, "I never use this item, and I am okay now without it. However, I might not be okay in the future, so I better keep it." If you have a lot of items that you are keeping for this reason, they can be a self-fulfilling prophecy that affirms a future filled with a lack of the things that you need.

As you clutter-clear, continue to ask yourself, "If this represented something about me and my life, what would it be?" When even one small thing is cleared, celebrate with enthusiasm. Honor yourself for what you have done. Stop. Breathe. Smile! Celebrate every advance that you make.

Day 6

Hi!

What a glorious morning it is here on the central coast of California! The blackbirds have arrived en masse to mate and give birth to their babies and then fly on. Last year, during a windy spring, I was constantly putting baby blackbirds back in their nests. (Yes, you really can do that—the mother won't reject them.)

Congratulations on making it this far! Today is more clutter-clearing. I know that I am having you do a lot of this, but there is a reason for it. Because objects are invested with meaning, clearing clutter has a direct effect on your psyche—when you shift the energy in your environment, it can have a mystical effect on your life.

In Tibetan Buddhism, it is believed that when you organize and clear your physical environment, then "drala" (or magic) can enter your life. If your space is messy and chaotic, then no drala will descend into it. When your life is not clogged with clutter, you feel lighter, and it is easier to hear the inner messages from your soul.

All my love,
Denise

P.S. Do what you can. Accept what you do not get done. Enjoy the process.

Day 6 *(Air)*: Lightening Up—Letting Go While Doing More Clutter-Clearing

There are many different kinds of clutter. Of course there is the usual home clutter, but there is also computer clutter (old files or documents in your computer that you will never use). Your purse can be cluttered with old receipts, dried makeup, used tissues, and so on. And your garden can be cluttered with overgrown or dead plants or piled trash.

But clutter can also be internal—for example, having such a busy schedule that you are always overwhelmed. Talking all the time without listening to others is also internal clutter. Always thinking, analyzing, rationalizing, or worrying, without taking time to be quiet and listen to your inner voice, is another type of internal clutter. Today is the time to address these other kinds of clutter.

Affirmation for the Day

"I am safe and centered no matter where I am."

Today

Take time to relax; listen to soothing music; and read inspiring quotes, poems, or passages. Take a walk. Breathe.

Overview

- *Committed to Change!*
  Level 1: Zen Teacup

- *Go for It!*
  Level 2: Schedule Time to Relax

- *Playing Full Out!*
  Level 3: Clearing Mental Clutter

Level 1: Zen Teacup

In Zen Buddhism, there is a famous story about a businessman and a Zen master. The businessman desires to become enlightened, so he visits the Zen master. The Zen master offers the businessman tea. He pours the tea into the cup and then keeps pouring until the tea is splashing on the floor.

The businessman becomes distraught and yells, "What are you doing?!"

The Zen master calmly replies, "This cup is like your mind: It is too full. It must be emptied first before you can attain enlightenment."

Take 15 minutes today to empty your mind. Create a quiet place to do this—if possible, turn off the ringers on your phone and eliminate other distractions. Sit still. Breathe. If you notice a thought, do not encourage it or deny it. Let it float by like a cloud. Become empty.

Level 2: Schedule Time to Relax

Take time to examine the schedule of your life. Have you scheduled time for joy, relaxation, and friends and family? As you look at the hours you spend devoted to different activities, what does the emphasis seem to be on?

There should be plenty of time for self-nurturing, pleasure, and relaxation. If there is not time for these things, make empowering choices today to eliminate nonessential aspects of your schedule. Make time in your daily planner or calendar for creativity, relaxation, and fun. *This is important!*

Cleave the shaft from the grain in your daily schedule. What could you delegate? What could you eliminate? Eliminate the activities that keep you in a constant state of busyness, and schedule time for joy. Please do this today.

Level 3: Clearing Mental Clutter

Today, begin to clear anything that might represent mental clutter (such as unnecessary papers, outdated files, old letters or Christmas cards, financial receipts, coupons, clipped articles, and so on).

Even though old files in your computer do not take up space, they can still be clutter if they *feel* like clutter. Also, be sure to back up anything on your computer that needs it. If a computer virus hits, it can be devastating, and worry over losing valuable computer files is mental clutter.

As you clear clutter, affirm: *"I am opening space within myself for remarkable mental clarity and focus."* As a suggestion, as you clutter-clear, you can say: *"With everything I release, more energy/love/abundance comes my way."*

If you only have time to clear one area, choose the area that will symbolically have the most impact on your life. For example, if you are experiencing blockages in your career, clear the desk in your office with the intent that you are gaining more mental clarity regarding your career.

‡ ‡ ‡

Day 7

Hi!
*Today is exciting because you have the opportunity to
begin to create a mission statement for your soul. I have
found this very important in my own life. My mission
statement gives me direction and clarity in uncertain times.*

*It is also a day to begin to watch for signs and secret
messages from the universe. I wish you the best on this
magical, thoughtful day—our last day of Air.*

All my love,
Denise

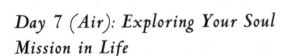

Day 7 (Air): Exploring Your Soul Mission in Life

You are here on the planet for a reason. There is
a purpose for your life. When you become clear about
your mission, a deep feeling of inner contentment begins
to develop within you. You truly know that every experience in your life is propelling you forward in alignment
with your mission.

Writing a mission statement that clearly and suc-
cinctly states your purpose can help bring a dynamic

clarity and focus into your life. When you write your mission statement or say it aloud, you should get an immediate rush of energy, strength, and vitality *because the words resonate with your soul.*

The words don't need to be fancy or eloquent or filled with ideals for humanity—they just need to be real and authentic. It may take hours to work on your mission statement, or it may come in a rush. Keep working with it until each word sings with your inner truth.

Today is also a day to watch for signs, synchronicities, and coincidences. In every moment, the universe is whispering to you. Even ordinary events in your life carry communications from the realm of Spirit. There are messages for you carried on the winds. There is wisdom in the morning songs of the birds. Even right now as you read this paragraph, you are surrounded by personal messages from Spirit.

Signs are powerful indicators that can give you understanding about yourself and insight about your direction in life. They can also reflect what is occurring in your subconscious mind. When you take time to listen to the whispers of the universe, you deepen your connection to your inner wisdom.

Affirmation for the Day
"Who I am is enough."

Today

Watch for signs, coincidences, and synchron-icities. Ask yourself the following about every experience today: "If this event had a message for my life, what would it be?"

Overview

- *Committed to Change!*
  Level 1: Ask "Why Am I Here?"

- *Go for It!*
  Level 2: Begin to Create Your Soul Mission Statement

- *Playing Full Out!*
  Level 3: Create a Soul Mission Collage

Level 1: Ask "Why Am I Here?"

Often the way that our soul talks to us is through synchronicities, coincidences, and signs. But most of us have lost our ability to listen to personal guidance available to us at every moment.

Today take time to listen to these secret messages. Ask yourself, "Why am I here?" and then watch for signs during the day. You might hear your messages through the "coincidental" songs played on the radio, through the conversations of the people next to you in line at the store, or through the spontaneous thoughts that pop into your head. When you take time to listen, valuable messages will show up in the most unexpected ways.

Level 2: Begin to Create Your Soul Mission Statement

Starting with the words: "The purpose of my life is . . . ," begin writing. Keep working on it until every time you say it, you can feel your entire being vibrate with joy. The soul loves the truth so much that when you state your true mission, every part of you expands with vitality and energy. It might take a while, and you may want to continue defining and refining your declaration about your soul's work during the weeks ahead.

In a way, your Soul Mission Statement engenders spiritual seeds. If you "plant" sweet corn or poison ivy, the universe will not distinguish or judge—it will give the energy freely for both to grow. So which seed do you choose to plant in the fertile soul of your soul? What do you want to grow?

Level 3: Create a Soul Mission Collage

On a large sheet of posterboard, write your Soul Mission Statement, and then either color, paint, or make a collage with pictures torn out of magazines to create a rendering of the "feeling" of your mission statement. For example, if your purpose in life is to "be joyous," then you would want to create a collage that gives you the feeling of joy.

Take this collage and put it in a place in your home (such as a bedroom wall), where it can serve as an affirmation of your alignment with your soul's purpose.

❖ ❖ ❖

Our Air Week has come to a close. Take a deep breath and a few minutes to reflect upon what you have accomplished, as your energy now shifts to the tasks of the new week: Water.

CHAPTER TWO

Water Week—
Clearing Your
Emotional Self

Several summers ago, I climbed up the hill that rises high on our land in Central California. From my vantage point I could see in all directions—from the rugged Santa Lucia mountains to the west, to the rambling vineyards that remind me of Tuscany to the south, to the stark Black Mountain which stands out from the grassy plains to the east. It was hot . . . *really* hot . . . the kind of heat that seems to suck the air out of your lungs when you inhale. And the persistent drone of the insects seemed like some forgotten ancient chant to me.

To the east, a storm was brewing. I watched as dark clouds rolled and tumbled down Black Mountain and lightning punctuated the darkening sky. The air smelled richly of earth and life. The wind picked up as the storm rapidly approached. It was exhilarating! Suddenly big raindrops began to pound the grasses.

I thrust my arms up to the heavens as cooling rainwater rushed down over my body and cascaded to the earth. As I opened my mouth wide to taste the wetness, my spirit was quenched. The rain seemed not only to be cleansing and replenishing the air and the land, but also purifying and renewing my soul.

Today we begin a new cycle by delving into the energy of the Water element. Water traditionally represents emotions, so this week is dedicated to clearing and cleansing the emotional self. Do not be concerned if emotional issues occur in your life during this week—all is not always as it seems. What occurs during this week can spur a deep, inner awakening . . . and it is all a part of the healing process.

This is the week where it is not uncommon to have emotional issues from the past surface. Remember that it is all a part of this grand clearing that you have embarked upon, and it is all good. You are letting go of old patterns that do not serve you anymore.

The Next Seven Days

When you first wake up for the next seven days, focus on the water around you and within you—your body is 75 percent water, and there is always water in the atmosphere. Even in the driest climate, there is still always some moisture in the air.

When you take a bath or shower, be aware of the cleansing and purifying aspect of water. Visualize negative patterns and thoughts spiraling away, down the drain. Imagine guilt, resentment, and fear swirling down through the plumbing.

Drink lots of water this week! Drink with the affirmation that the water is purifying your past, your body, and your soul. Also, while drinking the water, envision your body being hydrated and every cell absorbing the water and pushing toxins out of the body. Drinking water is one of the best ways to detoxify your body.

During Water Week

- Explore your emotional life.

- Cleanse your house, office, and car.

- Evaluate your relationships.

- Communicate from your heart, especially the things that you have been afraid to say.

- Encourage your inner child to play.

- Embrace your childlike wonder.

- Examine childhood issues.

- Explore your dreams.

- Follow your intuition.

- Bathe, shower, soak—cleanse your body.

- Check your plumbing (dripping faucets, clogged drains, and so forth).

- Run in the rain, roll in the snow, jump in a lake, and experience the spirit of water.

❀ ❀ ❀

Day 8

Hi!
Today is the first day of the Water Week. Water traditionally represents emotions, as well as purification and cleansing, so this is a week of clearing your emotions, your body, and your environment.
All my love,
Denise

Day 8 (Water): Exploring the Turning Points in Your Life

We all have emotions, and even the uncomfortable ones are the sweet juice of life. Imagine a symphony with only soft, lyrical music and no crescendo, or a movie where everyone is happy and peaceful throughout the entire two hours. It would be boring!

It is our emotions—sadness, exhilaration, fear, joy, grief, passion, and sense of adventure—that allow us to experience life in all its fullness and richness. If we cherish some of these emotions yet deny or suppress others, we are not balanced and whole.

Perhaps you know people who suppress their anger. There is a tension within them that is uncomfortable for everyone around them. When you own and honor all your emotions, there is a deep inner peace that arises within you. The soul loves the truth—so when you tell the truth about what you feel, you will experience inner peace.

It is also important to remember that although you *have* emotions, *you* are not your emotions. You are an infinite being, a child of the Creator, and a soul on a spiritual journey. Today you will be examining your life in the context of your emotions.

Affirmation for the Day

*"I unconditionally accept my feelings . . .
and what I feel is not who I am."*

Today

Connect with the spirit of water. When you drink, feel your body being hydrated and cleansed. Imagine that you are drinking rainwater or fresh, cold springwater. Cleanse your body with water. To do this, first dry brush your skin, then shower or bathe, and rinse with invigorating cold water. You'll step out of the shower/bath glowing!

<u>Overview</u>

- *Committed to Change!*
  Level I: What Were the Turning Points in Your Life?

- *Going for It!*
  Level 2: What Have You Learned During the Turning Points in Your Life?

- *Playing Full Out!*
  Level 3: What Are the Recurring Emotions of Your Life?

Level 1: What Were the Turning Points in Your Life?

In every life there are defining moments of insight, or experiences you have that cause you to make decisions that change your life. When you know what those moments are, you have an awareness of why you have made certain decisions in your life and why you continue to make these decisions. Awareness of these turning points means that you understand more fully why you do the things you do. If you do not know your turning points, life can seem random, unconnected, confusing, and even meaningless. It can give you a feeling that you do not know who you are.

A turning point can be a time when you made a disempowering decision that has determined everything that happened to you since, or it can be when you made an empowering decision that influenced your life afterwards.

Here is an example. At the beginning of my senior year in high school, I went to see Mrs. Peters, the school's career advisor, to get advice about what path to follow for my future. I told her that I wanted to go to college and become a psychologist to learn how to help people.

Mrs. Peters looked at me with a critical eye for a moment and then said that she did not think that I was cut out for college—especially not the psychology field. She said that I should think about finding a husband and getting married instead. I remember walking out of her office in a daze, my dreams for the future dashed. I walked to the river that meandered through town and climbed my favorite tree, which had big branches that loomed over the river.

I felt devastated. Yet, as I watched the golden-brown river flow beneath me, a resolve began to fill me. I thought, *No matter what she says, I am going to college! I will find a way to help people.* It was a turning point in my life.

Later, when I was faced with a multitude of obstacles that tried to impede my going to college, I kept seeing Mrs. Peters's critical face—I became absolutely determined that she was not going to be right about my future. Eventually, I made it to college. (I never did become a psychologist, but I like to think that my life's work *has* been helpful for others.)

To this day, whenever I encounter an obstacle, I remember Mrs. Peters, and an unbelievable determination spurs me to succeed, no matter what the odds.

Take time today to think about your past, and locate one of your own turning points. Write down the emotions that you felt during that pivotal time in your

Process Journal, and also note the decision that you made about yourself or about life based on that moment.

Level 2: What Have You Learned During the Turning Points in Your Life?

Continue the exercise above, but write down as many of the pivotal moments as you can. What decisions have molded your life? Additionally, write what you learned about yourself or about life during each of those times. Even if the event seemed like a negative one, really look to see what you gained or discovered about yourself as a result of that event.

Level 3: What Are the Recurring Emotions of Your Life?

Write down your life story, starting with what you know about your conception, your time in the womb, your early childhood, and so on (you can just jot the facts or use bullet points). As you write, note the primary emotions that you felt at different events in your life. For example, if you write, "At age four I got lost in the woods," you might write, "Terrified" (if that was what you felt at the time) next to it. Then ask yourself, "At that time, what decision did I make about my life?" An answer might be, "I decided that I was not safe on my own."

When you are complete with your list, go through it again, noticing the recurring emotions and decisions that you have made during your life. There are no wrong emotions—they are merely part of the juice of life. The problem occurs when we are stuck with one or two emotions and then rerun them over and over again.

For example, if you notice that there is a recurring theme of "resentment" throughout your life, this means that you are stuck on the merry-go-round of resentment. It is an emotion that is easy for you to call up at any given time. When you have a recurrent emotional pattern, there is a tendency to create circumstances to validate and reexperience that emotion because it is comfortable and familiar.

Be aware of how you are feeling doing this exercise. Continue to ask yourself today, "What am I feeling right now?" And no matter what you are feeling, affirm: *"I accept <u>all</u> of my emotions!"*

✣ ✣ ✣

Day 9

Hi!
I have been amazed at the synchronicity in nature while writing this book. When I was writing the Air days, the wind howled and great flurries whipped around my body whenever I took a walk. Also, the migrating black-birds arrived in great numbers.

As soon as I started to write about Water, the fog moved in and rain is in the forecast for tomorrow. I have always noticed these remarkable coincidences when working with the elements, but it never fails to move me. Today is an important day, so give it whatever time you can.

All my love,
Denise

Day 9 (Water): Examining the Meaning That You Give Your Life

We each have a personal history. And we give *meaning* to these specific events. We then choose to be happy or unhappy based on the meaning that we give our life experiences. What most people do not know is that they can *choose* the meaning they give all of their life circumstances.

For example, as I mentioned earlier, an unknown gunman shot me when I was 17. At the time, I thought that the reason this happened to me (and not someone else) was because I was not a worthwhile person—in other words, I deserved to be shot. Later in my life, I changed the meaning of that defining event. I decided that being injured so severely meant that I was able to learn about health and healing in a profound way that I never could have otherwise.

You are constantly giving meaning to the events of your life, so why not try to find ones that are empowering and do not cause you stress or anguish? For example, if someone honks at you and then cuts you off in traffic, you can decide that it means that the driver is a selfish lout or even that you did something wrong. Or you can choose to think that there is a reason for his actions, such as that he just heard that his wife is in labor and he wants to get to the hospital in time. You can either feel disgruntled or angry, or you can feel compassion. Since you have no way of knowing the motivations of that driver in that moment, choose a meaning for his actions that do not diminish you. Choose meanings for *your* life in the same way!

Affirmation for the Day

"My life experiences have positive, powerful meanings."

<u>Today</u>

Notice the meaning you give to everything that happens to you today.

<u>Overview</u>

- *Committed to Change!*
  **Level 1: Cleanse Yourself/Your Home/
  Your Car**

- *Go for It!*
  Level 2: Go to the Source of Meaning

- *Playing Full Out!*
  **Level 3: Changing Personal History—
  Make a Spirit Stick**

Level 1: Cleanse Yourself/Your Home/Your Car

Cleaning can be a mundane task or, if you employ the power of symbolic ceremony, it can be empowering and renewing. Today, choose an area in your home, such as a living-room window, to cleanse. As you clean it, affirm: *"I am letting more light into my life and into my soul"* and really *feel* more light and energy filling your life as you say the words. The more areas you can cleanse today, the more clarity you can bring into your life.

You can also choose to cleanse your body or a part of your body. For example, you can scrub your hair while saying: *"I am clearing my head of thoughts that do not empower me"* or (stated in the positive), *"I am clearing the way for positive uplifting thoughts to fill me."*

Level 2: Going to the Source of Meaning

You cannot always choose the circumstances of your life, but you *can* choose the meaning that you give those events. In your Process Journal, review your personal history and take time to be aware of the meanings that you have given your life. Pay particular attention to the events in which you experienced intense emotions.

Choose or locate one of the difficult or challenging moments from your life. To be aware of the meaning that you have given it, close your eyes and imagine that you are back at that time. Once you have visualized the event, go within. Travel inside yourself to the source from where "meaning" originates.

The significance that you give life comes from inside you. Go to the source of all the decisions that you make about life. Remember that *you* are the origin of everything that you decide about yourself and others. It is from this point that you can choose to keep the meaning you have given that event, or you can create a new meaning for it.

Level 3: Changing Personal History—Make a Spirit Stick

Ceremony and ritual have long been a part of the human condition because they allow us to project our thoughts, dreams, and desires into a conscious form. Creating a spirit stick can give clarity to the understanding of your life . . . it can even *change your life* or change your *perception* of your life.

A "spirit stick" is decorated for a particular purpose.

It can be decorated with items that symbolize your prayers for yourself or others. It can also be used to depict your life. Creating a physical symbolic depiction of your life can have a remarkable effect on your psyche.

Gregory had a very dramatic experience that was facilitated by the creation of a spirit stick. He came to me with the desire to heal his very strained relationships with his wife and two daughters. I suggested that he create a spirit stick to depict his life. First, he wrapped yarn and twine around his stick, and then he added shells and moss. Next, he placed a black bead on it to represent himself, a red bead for his wife, and two yellow beads for his daughters. When he was complete, he realized that he had placed his bead at a substantial distance from his family's beads and it did not feel right.

He spent several hours reworking his spirit stick until it *did* feel right. He put his bead much closer to the ones representing his family, and as he looked at it, he felt a sense of union with his family.

Remarkably, at the same time that he was reworking his spirit stick, his wife and daughters were discussing the family's dynamics. They concluded their discussion with a great deal of compassion and understanding for Gregory. When he returned home, it was as if a miracle had occurred—instead of the usual family discord, there was a wonderful sense of love and support all around.

As Gregory spent time focusing on his relationship with his family and began to change the meaning that he gave to his family dynamics through the creation of a spirit stick, almost magically his relationship with his family changed. So remember, *it is never too late to re-create your past.*

Create a spirit stick of your personal history that feels empowering to you. You can even give your life a sense of mythic proportions—by doing so, every time you look at your stick you reinforce the positive view of your past. You will need a stick, strips of fabric, and colored yarn or string (optional: feathers, moss, stones, shells, beads, leather, paper, and so on).

To make a spirit stick of your life, start with the bottom of the stick (your birth and childhood) and make a physical depiction of your life. Your present age is represented at the top of the stick. For example, if you were very quiet and subdued in your childhood, you might wrap a sedate colored blue yarn at the bottom of the stick.

Alternatively, create a prayer stick with objects that symbolize your prayers for either yourself or others. When you are complete, put it in nature for one day in a place where it can catch the early-morning sun. It is thought in some native traditions that the morning sun then takes your prayers to the Creator.

Decorate your stick in any way that you like. There is no set form. Use a small twig or a huge branch—it is up to you. When you are complete, look at it and notice how you *feel.* If you feel anything that is less than positive, change the meaning that you gave those events, and rework your spirit stick until you feel great looking at it.

‡ ‡ ‡

Day 10

Hi!

You have made it ten days! All I can say is "Hang in there!" Once you start a process of self-discovery, the forces of your life will propel you in the direction of your destiny. Even when you are not <u>doing</u> the program, you are still <u>on</u> the program. That is, even if you miss a day or do not do everything "right," you are still on the program. You are getting remarkable results, even if you are not consciously aware of them.

Do the best you can. Love, cherish, and accept yourself—and forgive yourself if it is not all done "perfectly." Doing this program perfectly is not the purpose of it. Know that you will get results no matter what you do (or do not do) between now and the end of this program. You have committed yourself to the Soul Coaching program, which is an act of power. No matter where life takes you in the next 18 days, in powerful and mysterious ways, the universe is working to connect you more deeply with your soul.

All my love,
Denise

Day 10 (Water): What Are Your Energy Zappers and Juicers?

In your life, there are people and patterns that deplete or "zap" your energy, but there are also people and places that uplift or "juice" your energy. The soul loves the truth, so when you identify your zappers, they have less of an effect on you. And when you identify the juicers, you can expand their presence in your life.

If something or someone is an energy zapper, take action today to minimize or eliminate this from your life. For example, if you think of making a trip to the grocery store and your energy goes down, see if they have a delivery service. You are not required to suffer in life. Alternatively, if something or someone juices you, then find ways today to increase their effect in your life.

Affirmation for the Day

"I am moving into harmony with everyone and everything in my universe."

Today

Notice the relationship you have with every person and every object you encounter. You do not need to change the way you relate . . . just be

> *aware of your energy. Does it go up or down, or is it neutral with each person and object?*

Overview

- *Committed to Change!*
  Level 1: Identify Your Energy Zappers

- *Going for It!*
  Level 2: Identify What Juices Your Energy

- *Playing Full Out!*
  Level 3: Commit Yourself to Diminishing One Zapper and Increasing One Juicer

Level 1: Identify Your Energy Zappers

An energy zapper is anything that lowers your energy and thus decreases your life force. Often you become so used to living with these zappers that you are not even conscious of their effect on you. Just becoming aware of them will begin to diminish their power. Throughout the day, notice what brings your energy down. Some examples might be:

- Always feeling exhausted after having been with a particular person

- Saying yes when you mean no

- Continually trying to please everyone

- Sitting in fluorescent-lit rooms with no windows

- Denying/suppressing what you are feeling

- Doing a task you do not enjoy

- Working all the time without taking time to rest and rejuvenate

- Watching excessive television

- Drinking too much alcohol

- Indulging in busyness on a consistent basis

- Not telling the truth

Write a list of your zappers in your Process Journal, and examine if there are any ways that you can eliminate or diminish some of them. For example, if one of your zappers is a family member that you cannot eliminate from your life, look to see if there are ways that you can diminish their effect on you. If they start to be really negative, you might say, "Hey, if we take a walk, you can tell me all about it." They may be just as negative on the walk, but you have diminished their usual effect on you because while they complain, you can look at trees and flowers, breathe fresh air, and get some exercise.

Level 2: Identify What Juices Your Energy

It is equally important to discover those things that uplift your energy. What juices your energy? Write it down. Some examples might be:

- Drinking hot tea while watching the sunrise

- Talking to a great friend

- Going for a walk

- Doing yoga

- Working in the garden

- Lighting candles at night

- Taking a bath with essential oils

- Sharing a wonderful glass of wine with a loved one

- Gathering with friends at a favorite restaurant
- Snuggling under the covers with a great book, or

- Lying in the grass and watching the clouds

Read through your list of juicers and see if there are any ways that you can increase or expand them in your life.

Level 3: Commit Yourself to Diminishing One Zapper and Increasing One Juicer

List the relationships that you have in your life now. In other words, *who* do you relate to on a regular basis? This list might include family members, friends, co-workers, neighbors, students, teachers, your hair stylist, life coach, auto mechanic, or grocer.

Now list *what* you relate to on a regular basis. It might be your car, food, cup collection, shop, garden, child's school, television, radio, computer, magazines, gym, or grocery store.

Use a scale from zero to ten, where zero is a real zapper, five is neutral, and ten is a real juicer. Go down each list, notice who or what brings your energy up and who or what brings it down, and give each item in your lists a number. Close your eyes and visualize the person or object, and notice how your body feels: Do you seem to feel more energy and vitality, or do you feel drained and exhausted? Some people or things might be neutral. In other words, they do not bring your energy up or down.

Make a commitment to change at least one zapper. For example, if your energy is zapped by watching excessive television, then make a commitment to watch less. Make plans to fill that time with something else. If you watch 21 hours of television a week, cut back to 10, and decide what you are going to do with those 12 hours a week that will juice your energy. You might decide to take a night class, start a hobby, read, or paint. Follow through on your commitment. Take action!

‡ ‡ ‡

D a y II

Hi! Today is the fourth day of Water Week, so do not be concerned if emotions are surfacing. Hang in there and let those emotions flow through you . . . it is all part of the energy of this week.

Hey, I am right in the thick of it, too. Yesterday I somehow ended up in the middle of a domestic fight between the woman who helps me clean my house and her husband, who happened to stop by. (My life is usually very calm—David and I have been married for almost 30 years, and we have rarely fought or disagreed with each other, so this was an event!) As the tears flew and these two yelled accusations at each other, I told myself how calm and centered I was amidst it all. (When you tell yourself over and over how calm you are, guess what? You are not really calm. When you are truly calm, you do not need to tell yourself you are. You just are.)

Although it is not uncommon for deep emotions to arise during Water Week, I asked myself why that particular experience had occurred for me. I suddenly realized that being "calm" was my defense mechanism when my parents had violent fights. I had unconsciously reactivated an old emotional pattern during Water Week to help heal any remnants of it.

You might find that during this program old patterns come up. This is good, as they are rising to the surface to heal and release. A great way to move through an emotion is to really feel it in your body and then exaggerate the feeling. In other words, feel it more. In fact, actually create the emotion.

You know that you are feeling an emotion because there are specific body sensations that you associate with each one. For example, you might know that you are feeling afraid because of a particular constricted feeling in your chest. What you resist persists, so instead of trying not to feel fear, choose to feel it. Create even more constriction in your chest and feel as much fear as you can. Exaggerate it!

A remarkable thing can happen as a result. As soon as you <u>do</u> an emotion rather than have it happen to you, it begins to dissipate. Tell yourself, "I am doing fear," "I am doing sadness," "I am doing worry," and so on. It can actually be fun—try it!

Today is another big day, for you are going to address relationships with yourself, others, and the Creator. I am sure that one of the main reasons we are here on the planet is to deal with relationships, for the way we relate to each other is ultimately a reflection of the way we relate to ourselves.

All my love,
Denise

Day 11 (Water): Exploring Your Relationships

The way we know we exist is through relationships. We have a relationship with our mother and father when we are born; then later with other family members, friends, and co-workers. We also have a relationship with animals, the elements of nature (rocks, sky, rain, fire, and so on), and with the Creator. We have relationships with household objects—our car, computer, and food—and even with money and sex. And, as I mentioned above, *the way you relate to every person, object, and thing is a reflection of the way you relate to yourself.*

When you begin to examine your relationships, you may find that the way you see the world around you is a reflection of the way others treated you when you were a child. If your parents were critical of you, you may have a tendency to be critical of others today. Your parents, however, are not to blame. They related to you the way that their parents related to them, and so on.

The way you relate with others and experience life is usually:

- a projection or a mirror of the qualities you suppress or do not accept within yourself,

- a reflection of the way people related to you when you were young, or

- a reflection of the core beliefs that you have about life.

Taking time to examine your relationships helps you understand and unweave negative relationship patterns.

Affirmations for the Day

"I am loved and lovable." "I love deeply and fully, and I am loved deeply and fully."

Today

Choose another area of your home to clean. If you do not know where to start, bedrooms, bedroom closets, and bathrooms are a good place. Clean that corner that you have not touched since you moved in. While you clean, say affirmations, such as: <u>*"As I clean, I am creating the space for new opportunities to flow my way."*</u>

Overview

- *Committed to Change!*
  Level 1: How Do You Relate to the World?

- *Go for It!*
  Level 2: Examine Recurring Relationship Patterns

- *Playing Full Out!*
  Level 3: Significant Relationships— Parents and God

Level 1: How Do You Relate to the World?

Today, be aware of the way that you relate to the world around you, and notice if there are any recurring emotional patterns. For example, my client Marion noticed that she had a recurring pattern of constantly protecting herself. She was not authentic with people because she was protecting herself from their judgments. The pattern was repeated in other areas of her life—she always checked several times to make sure that her car and house were locked, and she backed up every computer file three times.

The first step in the journey to your soul is telling the truth about where you are. Once you begin to notice your recurring emotional patterns, accept them and even love them. They have brought you to where you are now, and you have grown spiritually through having them.

The next step is to be willing to change those patterns. Patterns come from inner rules about life. But inner rules are just thoughts, and thoughts can be changed! To change your thoughts, create an affirmation to repeat over and over, such as: *"I am willing to release this pattern* [fill in what your particular pattern is] *and accept that I am safe and protected* [or whatever you would like to affirm]*!"*

An affirmation that is mumbled, routinely droned, or lazily chanted will not change anything. An affirmation that is shouted, visualized with emotional intensity, or said out loud with passionate body movements can and will change your life.

Level 2: Examine Recurring Relationship Patterns

Go through your life and examine the relationships that you have had in the past regarding these questions. (If a question does not address your relationship patterns, just skip over it.) Write the answers out in your Process Journal.

1. Have I had any negative recurring relationship patterns in the past?

2. Have those patterns healed, or are they still repeating in my present life?

3. If there was something that I could do to heal or resolve that relationship pattern, what might it be? (For example, you could accept it.)

4. What qualities do I consistently judge in others? (Often our recurring judgments regarding others say more about ourselves than about them. Also, the moment you judge someone, you lose the power to influence or help them.)

5. What do I need to communicate and to whom?

6. Is there anyone I need to ask forgiveness of or need to thank?

7. Is there anyone in my life I need to express love toward?

8. Is there anything for which I need to make amends? What is stopping me?

9. Is there a valued relationship in my past that faded away because I was afraid to tell someone something? What does it cost me if I tell

them? What does it cost me if I do not tell
them? What might I gain if I tell them? Am I
willing to take the risk?

10. Who or what do I need to forgive, accept,
or release?

11. Am I willing to let go of having to be right?

12. Do I unconditionally accept, with humor and
love, all of my relationship patterns?

13. Am I willing to release the *need* for those patterns?

To Change the World, Start with Yourself

Think of one person with whom you have been
uncomfortable or with whom you currently have a challenging relationship. Describe three things that you
would like to change about him or her, or three things
that you really do not like about that individual.

Now close your eyes and go into that authentic place
within yourself. Ask if there is any part of *you* that is a
reflection of those things that you dislike about this person. For example, Bob disliked Earl because Earl always
tried to dominate every conversation. However, when
Bob sought his internal truth, he realized that *he* tried
to control and dominate every conversation and did not
like it when anyone else did this.

To change the world, you need to change yourself first. Start
by being honest about yourself. There is no need for
guilt or blame, for these emotions will strip you of any
inner power to make changes in your life. Acknowledge

where you are and what is true, and you become open and receptive for life-transforming miracles.

Level 3: Significant Relationships—Parents and the Creator

You were molded by your parents. Even if your parents are not alive, you still have a relationship with them. Even if you were adopted, you still may have a relationship with your biological parents as well as your adopted parents. No matter whether you had a peaceful or a traumatic childhood, your mother and father and the events of your early childhood had an irrevocable effect on who you are. And it is beneficial to discover what that effect has been.

To uncover your authentic self, it is valuable to acknowledge that your beliefs about life are often a reflection of (or reaction to) your parents' patterns. You now have the opportunity to discover what *your* truth is.

Answer the questions below as honestly as you can. Remember, the way your parents treated you was programmed by the way they were treated.

1. If it is true that we choose our parents, why might I have chosen my parents? What have I gained or learned from having them as my parents?

2. How do I feel about them?

3. How do I perceive what they feel about me?

4. Is love flowing between me and my parents? If not, do I feel the need to heal this relationship? What do I need to do for this to happen?

5. What beliefs about life have I adopted from my parents? Are those beliefs an accurate reflection of what I know to be true?

If there are negative patterns that have passed down through your family's lineage, this is the time to break those old patterns so they are not passed down to your biological and spiritual descendants. Find a photo of each of your parents when they were children. (If you cannot find a photo, imagine them as children.) Look into the eyes of each one to see the soul within, and love that child as deeply and fully as you can.

※ ※ ※

Just as above, answer the following questions as truthfully as you can:

1. From who, what, and where do I get my spiritual inspiration?

2. What is my name for the Creator?

3. What do I want Spirit to know about me?

4. If I have conditions for Spirit in my life, what are they?

5. Am I willing to completely let go and allow Spirit to guide my life?

※ ※ ※

Day 12

Hi!

What a glorious yet bizarre day. The birds are singing and mating up a storm. Hawks are flying high overhead, and their whistles seem to echo through the valley. And cherry blossoms dance in the spring wind. At the same time, every 20 seconds I can hear the thundering roll of an explosion and fighter pilots are having dogfights over our house. It all seems so unreal. You see, there is a military camp about 45 minutes north of our home. It used to be an almost abandoned location that was primarily used for nature studies and the occasional National Guard exercise, but today it is being used for war games.

Our plumbing went out today. I guess this is part of my Water Week. All of this reminds me that everything that occurs this week is propelling us toward emotional clearing and helping us delve into sweet inner peace during these harried times. I know that the more inner peace we experience, the more we can effect peace in the world.

Once again, I would like to remind you to do what works for you. Enjoy the process, and celebrate what you have done. The program is not about perfection and completion; it is about being authentic, learning to listen to your soul's needs, and cherishing and loving yourself

May this day bring you closer to that precious place inside of you where your source waters run crystal clear and deep.

All my love,
Denise

Day 12 (Water): Being Still/ Doing Nothing

Your soul talks to you every day, but if you are too busy, you cannot hear what it is trying to say. Whether you are conscious of it or not, your soul is communicating with you. Signs, coincidences, synchronicities, and premonitions are the soul's kindly way of nudging you in the right direction. Use this day to begin to hear the heartfelt messages from your soul.

Affirmation for the Day

"In the center of my being, there is always stillness and peace."

Today

Remember the stillness in the center of the cyclone. No matter what is occurring around you, there is always an inner sanctuary of profound tranquility available to you.

Today, hold a glass of water in both your hands until the water becomes very still. Then slowly drink the water, imagining that it is cleansing you and filling your body with stillness and peace.

<u>Overview</u>

- *Committed to Change!*
  Level 1: Go Slow

- *Go for It Level!*
  Level 2: Watch for "Signs"

- *Playing Full Out!*
  Level 3: Do Nothing

Level 1: Go Slow

We often go so fast in life that we are out of touch with what we are really experiencing. When we slow life down, it is much easier to be in touch with what is authentic and real. Today, choose one activity, such as eating, walking, or breathing, and slow it way down. Spend 15 minutes going slow. If you choose eating, then chew very slowly, and cherish every nuance of flavor and texture of the food. Be aware of the way your teeth and tongue work together to chew, the way the food flows from your mouth into your stomach, and how your body immediately begins to utilize the nutrients in the food.

Level 2: Watch for "Signs"

Spend this day listening to the universe around you. Listen to the clouds, the sky, and the birds. Listen with your heart as well as your eyes. Be open to hear the secret messages around you. Write down what you receive today in your Process Journal.

When you encounter someone, instead of speaking to them immediately, take time to first listen to what *they* have to say. Be aware of the messages beneath their words. Look into that person's eyes, go beneath the personality to the level of the soul. What is their soul trying to tell your soul? That person is in your life today for a reason. What might that reason be?

Level 3: Do Nothing

It takes a certain amount of courage to truly do nothing. We get drawn into the hectic activity of life, but we also get drawn into the inner tangle of our constant thoughts, judgments, and evaluations. It can be an act of courage to simply sit still. Rest. Be. *Do nothing.* It can be one of the most difficult, courageous, and rewarding things a human being can do. Take at least an hour today to just Be.

☼ ☼ ☼

Day 13

Hi!

I am writing you as the sun rises into an eastern sky filled with robust, luminous pink clouds. I am feeling so thankful. I am appreciative for the sunrise, for my friends and family, and for all of the blessings in my life. I am also grateful to have lived long enough to be able to see my life in perspective. My wellspring of gratitude this morning is deep and wide.

Gratitude brings me closer to God than anything else I do. An added bonus is that the more I appreciate what I have, the more bounty is poured upon me. The more I criticize and judge what I have, however, the more my well runs dry.

Perhaps my prayers of immense gratitude this morning have their origins in the traditions of my Native American ancestors, who started each day with prayers of thankfulness. Even when it was cold, there was little food, or tragedy had struck the tribe, early morning was the time to be thankful for all the gifts they had. This kind of attitude about life brought my ancestors a feeling of peace and comfort.

Most Western-culture prayers are a supplication or an asking for something. This kind of prayer can sometimes bring discomfort, because it focuses on what you do not have or what you lack in life. It is not wrong; it is just a different way of praying. Today's assignment centers around a Native American concept—an "attitude of gratitude."

As I sit here in the glow of the sunrise, I am feeling so immensely grateful for the beauty of this morning. May this day bring you much joy.

All my love,
Denise

Day 13 (Water): Attitude of Gratitude

One of the fastest ways to reach into your soul is to surround yourself with an attitude of appreciation and gratitude. We get so busy in our lives that we forget to be thankful for all that we have and all that we are, yet gratitude is a key to happiness.

What you focus on in life is what you create. When you focus on what you are grateful for, you bring more of those things into your life. Yet when you focus on what you lack, you send a strong message to the universe that *you* are lacking, which becomes a self-fulfilling prophecy. And when you concentrate on how truly appreciative you are for what you have and for who you are, miracles abound.

Affirmation for the Day

"My life is blessed, and I am so grateful."

Today

Focus on what is great about every person you encounter and every experience you have today. What is wonderful about that person? What value are you gaining from that situation?

Overview

- *Committed to Change!*
  Level 1: Gratitude for Everything Today!

- *Go for It Level!*
  Level 2: What Are You Grateful for?

- *Playing Full Out!*
  Level 3: "I Love You. I Appreciate You."

Level 1: Gratitude for <u>Everything</u> Today!

From the moment you read this until you go to sleep, focus on what is good in every moment. Think about what you are thankful for in every situation. Today, let people in your life know what you appreciate about them or about what they are doing. Be sincere in your gratitude.

Level 2: What Are You Grateful for?

Write down what you are grateful for in your Process Journal. Then make a list of things that you are *not* grateful for. Now take each one of these and try to find a way that you could be grateful for it. For example, you might write, "I am *not* grateful for my divorce." But when you think about it, without your divorce you would never have known how strong you could be. So cross it out and write: "I am grateful for my divorce because I have become a stronger person. Now I can help others in a way I never could have before."

Level 3: "I Love You. I Appreciate You."

Look in the mirror and say, "I love you. I appreciate you." When I first tried this, it was extremely difficult! I had a hard time even looking at myself because I thought I looked so unattractive. To look in a mirror and say, "I love you, Denise" seemed like a big fat lie. And it was so embarrassing to look in a mirror and talk to myself. So I started by looking in the mirror and saying to myself, "I am willing to think about loving you, Denise." Somehow this didn't seem like a lie. I kept doing this exercise until I could finally say, "I love you, Denise." Now there are even some mornings when I wake up, look at myself in the mirror, and say "Hello, Gorgeous!" It is amazing how good it makes me feel.

If you have trouble with this exercise, find the words that feel true to you and then keep doing it until you can finally say, "Hello, Gorgeous! I love you!"

Day 14

Hi!

A soft fog has enveloped the small valley that I live in.
I seem to have been enveloped by water during this week.
Although the sun shines during the day, it has rained almost
every night. The moisture feels so cleansing and nourishing
to the land, as well as to my soul. However, I will be glad to
be entering Fire Week tomorrow, as Water Week has been so
eventful.

Our plumbing went out last night, and our yard and walk-
way are now torn up—this means all of my wonderful roses
have been pulled out. And now there is no running water in the
bathroom.

When the plumbers came, the sewer line erupted in the
house, and yuck sprayed all over the walls . . . I mean every-
where. Phew, it smelled bad! As I was cleaning it, the plumber
said, "Some of that s—t is 50 years old." Evidently, our 50-year
old plumbing had not been put in properly, so the sewage was
not all draining to the septic system.

I know that everything that occurs during Water Week
is helping me release old negative emotional blockages, so our
plumbing situation seems to be a powerful metaphor for my
life. Like the plumbing, I am more than 50 years old and still
dealing with emotional gunk from many years ago. These issues
had festered inside of me rather than moving out of my being,
like the sewage from our home that did not actually flow away
from the house. As I cleaned the walls, I affirmed: _"Old submerged emotional baggage is being cleansed and healed!"_

All my love,
Denise

P.S. You are halfway through the program.

Day 14 (Water): Releasing Victim Thinking / Choosing Your Life

Today is the last day of Water Week. It is potentially a powerful day—one where you can make choices that can have a huge impact on your life. Although we tend to think that "change" takes time, effort, and struggle, it can also occur in a moment. The moment you make a choice with absolute certainty and clarity, while cutting off all other pathways, your life irrevocably changes forever.

Today is also the time to start asking "noble questions", release victim thinking and consciously choose your life. Let's get started!

Affirmation for the Day

"Who I am is enough, just as I am."

Today

Find another area of your home to clean. Perhaps you could wash the windows, scrub the floors, dust the shelves, or wash the curtains. Clean with intention. For example, if you scrub the floor, you might affirm: "I am supported, and my foundations are clear and strong."

Overview

- *Committed to Change!*
  Level 1: Ask Yourself "Noble Questions"

- *Going for It!*
  Level 2: Release Victim Thinking

- *Playing Full Out!*
  Level 3: Choose Your Life

Level 1: Ask Yourself "Noble Questions"

Today, watch your thoughts and notice the number of questions that you ask yourself during the day. Some are simple, such as, "I wonder if I have time to make the bus?" or "Should I tell that woman she has spinach in her teeth?" However, you might notice some rather disturbing recurring questions, such as, "Why does this always happen to me?" "What is wrong with me?" "Why do I eat so much?" "Why am I unable to lose weight?" or "When will I ever learn?" These kinds of questions are not empowering.

Whenever you ask a question, the subconscious mind searches—almost like a computer—to find the answer. For example, if you ask, "Why do I always sabotage my relationships?" your subconscious will come up with an answer, such as, "You have lousy relationships because that is all you deserve" or some other nonproductive answer. It does not doubt the premise of your question; it just tries to find an answer.

These kinds of questions are called "unworthy questions." Whenever you ask yourself a negative or unworthy question, you will get a negative answer, which creates more negativity in your life. Negative questions thwart the opportunity to get a solution to a problem and keep you in a victim mode.

So today, whenever you find yourself thinking an unworthy question, I would like you to immediately replace it with a worthy or noble question. For example, if you find yourself asking, "Why did this happen to me?" immediately replace it with a noble question, such as, "What value can I get out of this situation?"

Noble questions can be better than affirmations because they lead to action, and once you are in action mode, you will feel that you are in control. You can even periodically create noble questions for yourself, such as, "How can I experience even more joy and love in my life right now?" Your mind does not doubt the premise that you are *already* experiencing joy, so your being responds by feeling good!

Your subconscious mind also begins to search for answers to your questions. For example, if you ask yourself, "How can I feel and be even more abundant?" your subconscious mind may come up with some fabulous creative ideas for you to become more prosperous. But if you ask, "Why am I always broke?" your subconscious mind will not doubt your premise that you are poor, and may give you an answer such as, "You are broke because you do not work hard enough!" which does not empower you.

Today, create one inspiring noble question to repeat over and over again. Some examples are:

- "How can I love and appreciate myself even more right now?"

- "How can I make a positive difference in the lives of those I love?"

- "How can I radiate even greater health?"

Level 2: Release Victim Thinking

"No one can make you feel inferior without your consent."
— Eleanor Roosevelt

Do you sometimes blame others for the difficulties in your life, or feel misunderstood, resentful, bitter, taken for granted, or underappreciated? If you answered yes to any of these questions, then you are allowing yourself to be a victim of life's circumstances.

The truth is that you are never truly a victim—unless you *allow* yourself to feel that way. You *always* have the choice to step beyond feeling victimized. Even when the situation seems to the world that you are a victim, you can choose the meaning that you give a situation.

When that man ran me down with his car and then shot me when I was 17 years old, it seemed to everyone, including me, that I was an innocent victim. The day I stopped feeling that way and changed how I viewed this event by seeing how much wisdom I had gained from this experience, I stepped into my power as a woman. When you choose *what is,* your word becomes law in the universe.

Today, imagine a situation where you feel or have felt treated badly or unfairly, and ask yourself the following questions. (As you answer them in your Process Journal, notice what emotions come up.)

1. "If there was something that I was gaining from this situation, what might it be?"

2. "Why am I allowing this person or situation to victimize me?"

3. "How can I change my perception of this event so that I don't feel victimized?"

4 "I have choices: Do I need to stand up to this person? Do I need to walk away? Do I need to change the context in which I view the situation?"

Level 3: Choose Your Life

It is an act of power to consciously choose your life. I do not mean to just choose parts of it (such as the parts you like or feel that you created), but to choose *all* of it—every bump, every dark night of the soul, every lie and falsehood, every fear . . . *everything.*

You step into self-mastery when you *own* your life—it allows you to *be here now.* To be fully connected with your soul, it is valuable to accept all that has occurred in your past. This helps you to stop living in the past so that you can be fully present here and now.

Tell the truth to yourself about your past, without suppression or denial. Own your past. Acknowledge what is about yourself and your life—without judgment, criticism, comparison, or hesitation. Every experience in your past has been an essential part of your spiritual journey.

Write out some of the pivotal events in your life (go to your list from Day 1), and after each one, affirm, *"I choose this experience, and I unconditionally accept this event in my life."* Keep saying it to yourself until you begin to *feel* unconditional acceptance of your life and your past.

Even if, deep down inside, you are kicking and screaming and saying that you did not choose that experience and you really were an innocent victim, know that just doing this exercise can have an empowering effect. It can help you step out of the victim mode and into your majesty as a spiritual being.

‡ ‡ ‡

Our Water Week has come to a close. Take a deep breath and a few minutes to reflect upon what you have accomplished, as your energy now shifts to the tasks of the new week: Fire.

CHAPTER THREE

Fire Week—
Clearing Your
Spiritual Self

Last summer there were lots of fires in the rural area where we live. One morning, my husband and I were awakened by the smell of smoke—our neighbor's property was aflame! After calling for the fire department, we climbed a hill a safe distance away and watched as courageous firefighters successfully battled the flames, and planes swooped low to drop huge buckets of water on it.

Now, many months later, it is spring and the land is alive with wildflowers. Even the old-timers say it is the most beautiful display they have ever seen. Areas blackened by the fires of last year are now covered with huge masses of yellow, purple, orange, and blue blooms.

In nature, fire has the ability to dramatically clear a landscape, yet the aftermath is new growth. Old brush is cleared away so that sunlight and moisture can reach the land for new life. During Fire Week, do not be surprised if you experience a powerful inner clearing. Tapping in to your spiritual light often entails facing your darkness, so anger and irritation may come up this week. This is not bad—these emotions are rising to the surface so that they can be released. Fire is also related to your life force, the spark of life and pure light within you. Additionally, it represents vitality, action, movement, taking risks, transformation, and change.

This is also the week that many breakthroughs occur. This is also the time to begin to change old, limiting patterns and habits. Routines and habits can lock you into repeating negative cycles in life. Often we react to situations because of preconditioned responses based on outmoded ideas about ourselves, rather than the true yearnings of our soul. So even tiny modifications in your routine, such as changing what you have for breakfast, can help you begin to transform your definition of self.

One of the most important ways to change your life is with action. We often hesitate to take action because of fear—fear of success, fear of failure, or even deeply buried subconscious fears. Fire week is the time to objectively look at your fears and to also take action to overcome them. And do not be surprised if unexpected events or spiritual insights occur during this week. No matter what form they take, they will contribute to your stepping into an expanded energy within yourself.

The Next Seven Days

Each morning during this week, focus on the fire around you and within you as soon as you wake up. Light is an aspect of fire, so if there is any sunlight in your bedroom, imagine that you are breathing in its light and power. Focus your awareness on the interplay of light and shadows in your surroundings. Be aware of fire in all its aspects throughout each day for the entire week. By doing so, you are activating the Spirit of Fire that dwells in and around you.

During Fire Week

- Step into trust and faith.

- Meditate on your inner light.

- Listen to any inner voices urging you to branch out in new directions.

- Change your routines and habits.

- Take risks.

- Activate creativity.

- Access your spiritual allies.

- Face your shadow self.

- Examine your fears.

- Have fun!

‡ ‡ ‡

Day 15

Hi!

Whew! I am glad to be into Fire Week to "dry out." Water Week was eventful for me—lots of old emotional patterns surfaced, and sometimes it was hard to ride that emotional wave. However, just when I thought it would be great to be out of Water and get into Fire, the tractor that was tearing up our yard today (to change the plumbing that broke during Water Week) tore through the electrical lines, so our electricity is now out. (I equate electricity with fire energy.) Well, it will be interesting to see what happens this week.

Fire Week is the time to wake up the spirit! To do this, move your body. All the submerged emotional baggage that got stirred up in Water Week can now shift out of your energy field with the powerful activation of fire. This is the week of spiritual purification, facing fears, releasing anger, and taking action. It is easier to dissolve the blockages of your spiritual self if you move your body. So this week: Dance. Run. Walk. Exercise. Move!

All my love,
Denise

Day 15 (Fire): Confronting Fear / Developing Faith

As a child, I was afraid of so many things: I was afraid of my mother's violent rages and my father's simmering undercurrents, and I was scared every time I started a new school (we moved nine times when I was a child). Then, when I became an adult, fear continued to shape my life. I was afraid of failure, but also afraid of success. I was afraid of being rejected, and also afraid of being loved. Most of the major decisions I made in my life were based on fear. But now I am unraveling my fears, understanding my shadow self, and learning about the person who exists beneath the fear.

On your journey to the soul, it is valuable to explore the dark hidden crevices within your psyche. This is the place that famed Swiss psychologist Carl Jung called the "shadow self"—the part of you that is denied or suppressed because it makes you uncomfortable or afraid. Jung asked, "Would you rather be good or whole?" Many people choose being nice and sacrificing their needs for others, and as a result, they are fractured.

It is especially important to explore your fears as you strive for the light. As you understand and own your fears, they have less power over you because in life what you resist persists. Resist your fears and they become even stronger; acknowledge their presence and even accept them, and they will relinquish their hold on your life.

<u>Affirmation for the Day</u>
"I am safe."

<u>Today</u>

Be aware of all the forms of fire in your life—from the sun, to candlelight, to fire, to the inner light within you. Imagine breathing in the energy of sun today.

<u>Overview</u>

- *Committed to Change!*
  Level 1: Acknowledge Your Fears

- *Going for It!*
  Level 2: Take a Risk

- *Playing Full Out!*
  Level 3: Take Action!

Level 1: Acknowledge Your Fears

It is an old expression, but a true one, "A fear named is a fear tamed." In other words, as you acknowledge that which you are afraid of, it has less power in your life.

In your Process Journal, list the things that you are afraid of. Write: "I am afraid of . . . ," and be as specific as possible. No fears are better or worse—they are just fears, and they are *not* who you are!

After you have written your list, choose your biggest fear and imagine a worst-case scenario regarding it. Then find a way that you could survive and even thrive if this were to happen to you. For example, at one time my client Sue's worst possible fear was to have a lack of freedom through being confined or incarcerated. When she did this exercise, she tried to think of how being in confinement could be a valuable or positive experience.

It was not easy for Sue to think of anything positive at first. Then she realized that she could actually be a valuable asset to the other people in prison. She could help women who otherwise might not have been able to be helped. When she thought of this, she was no longer afraid of confinement. (Of course no one *wants* to be confined, but what was important was that Sue was not so afraid of it anymore.)

Remember, the road to success is often paved with failure. Being willing to take a risk means being willing to fail. Dr. Seuss (Theodor Geisel) was ready to burn his first manuscript because it was rejected by 27 publishers, but he never gave up and went on to have many bestsellers. So take some risks! Be willing to fail. Unleash yourself upon the world!

Level 2: Take a Risk

Today, start taking little risks. Push out of your comfort zone just a bit. Choose one of the fears from your list and take a tiny step to face it, overcome it, or release it. For example, if you are terrified of public speaking, ask your family (and maybe even a few friends) to gather while you give a small presentation.

Or if you wear large, oversized clothes because you are overweight and afraid to let anyone see your body, go shopping in a blouse that is not oversized. Every time you take a small step toward facing a fear, your confidence will grow.

Level 3: Take Action!

One of the most important things that you can do to change the quality of your life is to take action. You already know what is working and what is not working in your life. You have read self-help books and listened to lectures—you know what you need to do. Today, take substantial *action* on one of the areas you fear. Begin now!

Fear is what stops most of us from stepping into our light. Everyone feels fear; it is a normal part of being alive. And it never goes away. As long as you keep pushing up against your own limitations, you will have fear. But as long as you keep expanding your personal parameters, it becomes easier and easier to experience fear and yet step forward anyway.

My client Helen took action to confront her fear of rejection. She had written poetry for years and had always wanted to have her work published, but she had never submitted anything to a publisher. Helen realized that this was because she was afraid of being rejected—so she decided to take a risk and send some of her work to a poetry magazine. Although she *did* eventually receive a rejection notice, she said that it did not matter because of the elation that she felt at having finally taken action. She is now submitting her work to lots of magazines. She feels that finally taking action has had a positive effect in other areas of her life where she also had a fear of rejection.

⚜ ⚜ ⚜

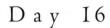

Day 16

Hi!

Fire energy is lively. It ignites enthusiasm and excitement. Today is a fun day! It is a day to take risks and begin to see the world through new eyes. The fact that our yard is torn up, the plumbing is out, and there is no electricity is forcing me to see the world through "new eyes." May your life also be a great and grand adventure.

All my love,
Denise

Day 16 (Fire): Taking Risks

If you do what you have always done, you will get what you have always gotten. In other words, if everything stays the same, nothing changes.

Discovering your authentic self means being willing to step into the unknown. It means being willing to do things in a different way. We all fall into old patterns and habits, some of which are a result of protecting and defending ourselves from failing, being hurt, or humiliated.

Sometimes, on the journey to discover your soul, you might encounter some failures, but remember the

Japanese proverb "Fall down seven, get up eight." In other words, when you make your decision with faith, and keep on going no matter what.

Affirmation for the Day

"I am free to experience joy in every moment . . .
no matter what is happening in my life."

Today

Constantly ask yourself, "How can I experi-
ence even more joy and fun today?" and see what
your subconscious comes up with!

Overview

- *Committed to Change!*
  Level 1: Fun!

- *Going for It!*
  Level 2: Step Out of Your Comfort Zone

- *Playing Full Out!*
  Level 3: Break a Habit Today

Level 1: Fun!

No matter what is happening in your life today, find a way to create *fun* and joy while doing it. If you have to run errands all day, ask yourself how you could enjoy yourself while you do them. Perhaps you could play some hot salsa music on your CD player and rock out in your car at the stop signs. Or maybe you could belt out a song at the top of your lungs while you soar along the highway. (My car is one of the only places where I can sing as loud as I want to without worrying about other people's reactions.) List in your Process Journal what is really fun for you. Continue to ask (and answer) today's question: "How can I experience even more joy and fun right now?"

This next exercise involves taking a risk, but it is one of the fastest ways to break out of old behavioral modes: Laugh yourself silly! Don't just giggle, laugh with the exuberance of a child. Even if you do not really feel like laughing, pretend to have a huge belly laugh. Roll on the floor guffawing. Snort when you laugh. When was the last time you had a cackling, chortling, falling-down-laughing fit? Never? Why not start today. Even pretending can have an amazing impact on your soul. Hey! Come on. Really do it! You have nothing to lose . . . and everything to gain.

Level 2: Step Out of Your Comfort Zone

Today is the day to step out of your comfort zone. I have heard of remarkable research in the Netherlands in which cancer patients were asked to completely change their routines, hairstyles, clothing style, and so on—all of which deeply shifted the way they saw themselves and life. Remarkably, there were much higher levels of spontaneous remissions in this group than in the test group. The theory is that their outer changes affected their inner selves.

So make a change for today. Surprise people! Surprise *yourself!* Be unpredictable—change your hairstyle, makeup, or clothing style (bring out the leather jacket or the prim dress). Walk barefoot in the snow . . . heck, roll in it, and throw handfuls of it in the air. If you are always early, be late. If you are always late, be early. Light some candles, dance naked sensuously and slowly or fast and erotically. Do something—anything—that is out of character for you.

Breaking out of your self-imposed rut can help you dispel any solidifying of your identity that keeps you from connecting to the soft sweetness of your soul.

Level 3: Break a Habit Today

We all have habits. Although they tend to make our lives easier, our habits and routines do sometimes limit us. Do you remember when you were a kid and a day lasted forever and a week was an eternity? It was because everything was a new and exciting experience; you did not have routines to fall back on.

Examine your life: Are there any habitual behaviors that do not support the needs of your soul? For example, do you habitually watch four hours of television a day? What can you do today (and in the future) to change some of the habits that do not empower you?

❦ ❦ ❦

Day 17

Hi!

Well, I believe in miracles! Yesterday our yard was torn up, and you would not have wanted to be downwind, because it was really bad—50 years of sewage aromas were wafting through the air!

Then two men showed up and asked if we had some work for them. They were like angels arriving at a time of need.

Along with my husband, they literally shoveled sewage all day into wheelbarrows to transport and bury at a distant location. I could not help with the shoveling, although I was a great cheerleader! (It was the one time I was really glad to have a writing deadline.) At the end of the day, everything was done—I poured some wine, and we all celebrated!

I really think it is important to celebrate after you have accomplished something. I hope that you are taking time to celebrate the insights that you are gaining, the clutter that you are clearing, and the commitments that you are keeping as you do this program. Even if it is a tiny step forward, celebrate it! This will actually help you grow faster, because then you will have a conditioned behavioral response that equates spiritual growth with celebration and joy rather than with suffering and struggle.

Okay, if you are saying to yourself, "I have not really been doing the program, so I might as well quit," it is too late. Once you made the commitment to start this program, it started to work in your life, even if you have not done a single exercise!

How can I say this so boldly? Well, I have received amazing e-mails from hundreds of people who wrote to tell me that even though they had not been doing the program exactly according to the directions, they still had powerful healing experiences that amazingly seemed to coincide with the program. So instead of bemoaning what you did not accomplish, celebrate what you _did_ do, no matter what it was. And recommit to the commitments you made on Day 2.

The results of this program do not necessarily come from how much you do—they come from your intent and your commitment to listen to the yearnings of your soul.

All my love,
Denise

P.S. I just went to make a cup of tea, and the electric teapot that I have had for ten years just blew up. I mean literally blew up, with a huge spark and smoke! I think I am being spurred into action for Fire Week. We have also spent a good part of the last two days with the electrical company discussing high-voltage wires that are going to be put across our land. More Fire!

Day 17 (Fire): Facing the Shadow

We all have parts of ourselves that we do not want to acknowledge or that we do not want to take responsibility for. This is our "shadow self." Often we are so disconnected from our darkest inner realms that the only way we can find those parts of ourselves is through "projections," which occur when we subconsciously cast our shadow to the world around us and then it reflects back to us. For example, someone who constantly encounters hostile people wherever they go usually has a shadow self filled with suppressed hostility, even if they say they never feel hostile themselves.

It is immensely important to be honest with yourself about your shadow self. If you want to see the nature of your shadow, be aware of your judgments about others. If you *observe* something, it is not a projection, but if you *judge* it, it is. What you judge in others can be a reflection of qualities that you possess but deny within yourself.

In other words, if I am upset with someone else's selfishness/rudeness/condescending nature, it is usually because I am not accepting these qualities within myself. So I need to look carefully within myself to see if (1) I have exhibited these qualities in the past, (2) I am doing so now, or (3) I have the capacity to demonstrate these in the future. When I have accepted these qualities within myself, I will not be so deeply offended by others displaying these tendencies.

Today's processes are aimed at beginning to own all the parts of yourself and to take responsibility for the choices that you make in life. This will help you become more whole, as you accept and honor both your darkness and your light.

Affirmation for the Day

"I unconditionally accept all parts of myself."

Today

Be aware of every time you negatively judge someone or something, then ask yourself, "Could this trait possibly be something that I have exhibited in the past, am currently exhibiting, or am capable of manifesting in the future?" Just examining your judgments begins to allow an integration to occur.

Overview

- *Committed to Change!*
  Level 1: Replacing "Could" for "Should"

- *Going for It!*
  Level 2: Letting Skeletons Out of the Closet

- *Playing Full Out!*
  Level 3: Move Your Body and Move Your Soul!

Level 1: Replacing "Could" for "Should"

Self-criticism is part of the shadow self. It is the part that tells you that you should do something, and then causes you to feel guilty or ashamed because you are not doing it. Today, make a list of all the things that you should do. Then take each item and ask yourself these questions:

1. "Who says I should?"

2. "Why should I?"

Let your mind brainstorm for a bit and see if there are any childhood memories or associations regarding this "should." Is it *your* "should," or did it come from someone or somewhere else?

Now write the list again, and this time, change "should" for "could" and after it write: " . . . but I choose not to at this time." For example, the sentence "I 'should' immediately respond to every letter and e-mail I get," becomes "I 'could' respond to every letter and e-mail I get immediately, but I choose not to at this time."

The truth is, you probably could respond to every letter right away, but you choose not to. "Should" implies guilt, so when you truly take responsibility for your actions, you gain freedom by telling yourself the truth.

Level 2: Letting Skeletons Out of the Closet

Our lives are determined by the past, especially the past that is forgotten or denied. And almost everybody and every family has secrets from the past. But left dormant, these experiences can still cast long shadows that can darken your future.

Secrets take on a life of their own. They create "territories of the unspoken," with tacit rules that those subjects can never be discussed. They dampen the human spirit and make it harder to hear the soul. Did you have any family secrets with which you grew up? Is there anything about yourself that you do not want anyone to know? Is there anything that you have been harboring about someone else that weighs on you? Is there something that you have done that you feel ashamed of and have never told anyone? The answer to all these questions might be no, but if there is a yes, write out the secret. Look at it, and then ask, "So what?" As you do, notice what memories, thoughts, and energy shifts occur within you. Just objectively examining your secrets begins to diminish some of the effects that they have on you.

Also, if you are really "Going For It!" then I suggest that you consider taking a risk and telling your secret to someone you trust. You'll be surprised how good it can make you feel.

Recently I was with my friend Amber on a late-night cross-country drive through the desert during a pounding rainstorm. As we careened through the waterlogged road, I told her something that I was so ashamed of I had never told anyone else. I felt so humiliated to even say the words out loud.

She said, "That's it?" Then she started to laugh, and she was soon howling with laughter.

I started to laugh, too. *Hey,* I thought, *so what?!* In that moment, my deep shame dissolved.

Level 3: Move Your Body and Move Your Soul!

So you've decided to "Play Full Out!" today—great! Here are your assignments. First, in your Process Journal, write down your sexual history. Describe your first sexual awakenings—write about the good times, the bad times, early childhood memories—everything. As you write, continue to notice what emotions and memories surface. Write down your feelings regarding all of those events. Remember that although you have a sexual past, you are *not* your past. The past does not need to equate to the future.

Next, write about a day in the future when your relationship with your sexuality is great. Write it as if the future has already happened. For example, write: "The year is 2015. I am lying in bed with my lover of the past several years, and we are enveloped in each other's arms," or "The year is 2012; I live alone and I love it! Although I do not have a long-term partner, I feel so balanced regarding my sexuality and sensuality."

The second assignment is to take at least 30 minutes in order to "dance your darkness and dance your light." Put on music in which you can lose yourself. Before you begin, close your eyes and recall if there is any part of you that is shame-ridden, guilty, pitiful, bitter, resentful, disgusted, bitchy, or mean-spirited. Then imagine that quality blown way out of proportion, and dance that quality. Do the "Mean Dance," the "Guilty Dance," and so on. Really move your body, and dance as if you were totally embodying that quality. If you have several shadow qualities, dance them all at once, or one at a time. If you get exhausted, dance through the exhaustion. Keep going, no matter what.

Then stop, close your eyes, and think of all the special qualities you embody, such as joy, kindness, compassion, charity, graciousness, and love. Now embody these qualities, dance each quality as your entire being embraces the quality, and keep going until you can feel it in every pore of your body.

⚜ ⚜ ⚜

Day 18

Hi!

When I woke up this morning, I was thinking about today's exercise regarding being in the present moment. This exercise really helped me when I was diagnosed with breast cancer. During that time in my life, I was scared about the pain I might have to go through in the future, and I was also worried about my daughter and husband potentially living without me. I lived in the past, with regretful thoughts such as "I should have exercised more or eaten better," or I worried about the future with thoughts such as, "David will be so sad without me." Regretting the past or worrying about the future was nonproductive. It did not change my situation, and it did not empower me.

When I would stop and ask myself, "Hey, what is true for me right now?" I would then realize that the truth was that I was not in pain and I was not dead . . . and I would recognize that there was a lot to be happy about. I would find immense joy in the smallest events. As long as I stayed in the present moment, I was happy. Today's exercise can help you be present here and now.

I wish you my best on this glorious day!
All my love,
Denise

Day 18 (Fire): Being Present / Saying Yes to Life

In truth, the only thing that we have is the present, since the past is gone and the future is still to come. Yet we spend so much time in the past and the future that we very rarely take the opportunity to experience the delight available in the present moment.

When I was diagnosed with cancer, it was so easy to live in the past with thoughts such as *Why I did I not take better care of myself?* And it was also easy to live in the future, with fear about people judging me for getting cancer and also fear of the pain and suffering that the cancer might bring.

Then one day I woke up and asked myself, "What is true in this moment?" The truth was that I was alive, with a splendid day ahead of me to experience in any way I chose. I could choose to plunder through that day with regret about the past and worry about the future, or I could cherish every experience that life brought me. Everything seemed to flow from that point—I experienced such radiance and joy. That moment was a turning point that I believe eventually, helped lead to my deliverance from cancer.

<u>Affirmation for the Day</u>

"I invite the pure light of the sun into my heart.
May it shine from my heart to the world."

<u>Today</u>

Sit before a candle, inhale, and imagine breathing in the spirit and life force of fire. Visualize the purifying energy of fire surging through your entire being, burning any impurities within you.

<u>Overview</u>

- *Committed to Change!*
  Level 1: Being in the Present Moment

- *Going for It!*
  Level 2: Trust and Faith

- *Playing Full Out!*
  Level 3: Saying Yes to Life!

Level 1: Being in the Present Moment

When you are totally in the present moment, you do not experience stress. You become stressed when you either replay the past or worry about the future. If you are constantly thinking, *What if I can't handle* [fill in the blank]? *I am afraid that* [fill in the blank] *might happen,* or *What did she mean when she said that?* you are not fully experiencing the joy that is available in the moment.

Today, continually ask yourself, "What is happening *right now,* in this moment?" For example, my client Sarah did this exercise when she was eating pizza, and she said that it actually tasted better because, instead of thinking of the next bite as she usually did, she fully experienced the contrasting flavors and textures of the pizza. She also ate less because she was aware of when she was full.

Take time today to sink into your truth. Often we are so busy living in the future or fretting over the past that we miss the immediate joy that is available in the present moment. If you find your mind wandering, gently say to yourself, "I cannot change the past, and tomorrow is not here. All I need is within me right now."

Level 2: Trust and Faith

Within you is divine light, pure and radiant. Close your eyes and gently encourage your body to relax and your mind to become still. Imagine yourself on a sunny seashore. An angel of light floats down with golden wings and gently wraps them around you.

Imagine yourself sinking into a feeling of deep surrender, relaxation, and infinite trust and faith as you are gently rocked and held by the angel. You know that you are loved. You know that you are enough just as you are. You know that the light within you is expanding and becoming even more vibrant and glowing. Take at least ten minutes to do this, and write down what you experienced in your Process Journal.

Level 3: Saying Yes to Life!

Your inner fire energy is your vitality, spontaneity, creativity, and life force. It is the part of you that says yes to life. When you can say yes to life in one area, it creates an opening for new energy, new ideas, and new inspiration in other areas.

Today, from the moment you wake up, choose your life. Choose every experience. Say, "Yes, this is what I want right now!" Even if it feels forced or uncomfortable, do this for a day. The most difficult situations can be filled with blessings if you look for them.

Maybe you cannot change all the experiences you have today, but you can certainly choose your reaction to them. Even if it feels silly, act as if everything that happens today is a special gift to you from the Creator, filled with meaning and blessings. Say, "This, too, is a part of the Creator's plan for me today." And tell yourself that no matter what happens, you will find a way that this day can be great!

Tonight, write down the events of your day in your Process Journal, and reflect on the many blessings that have come into your life today.

❦ ❦ ❦

Day 19

Hi!

Today is a cut-to-the chase day: It is a fun, thrilling, potentially challenging day to really face your death.

When I was diagnosed with cancer, one empowering thing I did was to completely accept the fact that I might die. As strange as it sounds, it was an exhilarating experience. I felt such a sense of freedom when I embraced my possible death—I felt free to stop living for everyone else and start living for myself.

I am still not exactly sure why the doctors could not find any trace of cancer later (they said they must have made a mistake in their first diagnosis), but I am sure that accepting my life (and my death) in every moment helped free my body from cancer.

I do know that in order to live fully, it is important to embrace and accept death. Today's exercises are all about this.

All my love,
Denise

Day 19 (Fire): Facing Your Death / Embracing Your Life

It has been said that a brave being dies only once, but a coward dies a thousand deaths. There is truth in this—but what is not said is that one of the ways to become brave is by facing and honoring death.

Although *you* will never die, your body most certainly will. To the extent that you identify with your body (and not with your soul), the death process will be frightening and filled with emotional distress. Yet if you accept death as a valuable part of your evolution as a soul, then you will be able to fully live in the present.

Affirmation for the Day

"I live in the present moment with courage and love."

Today

Cherish your life and embrace your death. And cherish life and death in all its forms. Notice the fallen leaves as well as the new sprouts pushing through the earth, and remember that without death, there cannot be life.

OVERVIEW

- *Committed to Change!*
  Level I: Make a Ceremonial Fire

- *Going for It!*
  Level 2: Rocking-Chair Test

- *Playing Full Out!*
  Level 3: Practice Dying

Level 1: Make a Ceremonial Fire

Rituals and ceremonies speak the language of the soul. During a sacred ceremony, energy is generated that opens your heart and soul, which makes you more accessible to your inner truth and to the Creator.

Today, make a ceremonial fire. It can be a candle, a flame in a metal bowl, a fire in a fireplace, or an outside campfire. In this fire, place something that represents your body or your past identity. (You can use a piece of paper with a drawing of your body or of something that represents your identity.) As it burns, say, "Although I have a body/identity, it is not who I am. In my essence, I am Divine Light." Focus on the flame as you do this.

Level 2: Rocking-Chair Test

I am of Cherokee heritage on my mother's side. Many Native Americans have an expression that I love—"It is a good day to die." To me, this expression means, "I accept my life in its totality. I accept who and what I am. I am complete right now. If I am to die today, I am ready."

Are *you* ready to die today? If the answer is no, why not? Is it because you have not completed something or have family to care for? Or is it because you do not feel that who you are is enough?

I am not always ready to die. Some days I get caught in the illusion that I am not enough—or I have not grown enough, succeeded enough, or learned enough— and I just do not feel ready to die. But on the days that I *am* ready, a sacred inner peace pervades me, and I feel complete and whole in every moment.

Imagine that you are sitting in a rocking chair, reviewing your life at the end of your days. Answer these questions honestly and from your heart:

1. Are you ready to die?

2. Do you feel complete and at peace with the life you have lived?

3. If not, what would you have liked to have done differently?

4. What would you have done less of and what would you have done more of?

You have a limited number of years, months, weeks, and days until you die . . . so how can you make the most of the time you have left? What are your priorities? What have you been putting off?

Keep in mind that the first and most important step in transformation is *action.* So what action can you take today so that when you are at the end of your days, you can be absolutely satisfied that you lived life to its fullest? Make a plan to take that action.

Level 3: Practice Dying

One technique athletes use to improve their skill is to visualize a performance over and over again. For example, competitive downhill skiers will often visualize themselves doing a ski run over and over again, which tends to dramatically improve their performance.

To overcome the fear of death and even embrace it, it is valuable to practice dying. Of course this does not mean actually dying—it means that you just imagine your body dying over and over again until *you no longer feel afraid*.

This can actually be a fun exercise—remember in childhood plays how everyone always wanted to act out the death scene because the drama of it was so exciting? Visualizing yourself dying can be fun. Try out different kinds of death, from intense fatalities such as falling off a cliff, having a heart attack, drowning, or being in a car accident, to less dramatic passings from cancer, or even dying in your sleep. Get into the drama of it.

Every time you imagine yourself dying, also visualize slipping out of your body and going to a place that is exquisitely beautiful and peaceful. It might be a garden or a gentle meadow, or it might be a place where angelic beings or people who love you are waiting for you with open arms.

The more you can accept and even embrace the fact that your body will die, the less the fear of death will subtly penetrate into your everyday life. The less fear of death you have, the more fully you can live in the present moment.

☙ ☙ ☙

Day 20

Hi!

You only have eight more days to go. Don't give up. Keep going! Do the best you can. Remember that you started this program for a reason. There was something in your life that you were yearning for. Remember why you started and know that enlightenment and transformation can happen in an instant.

When I lived in a Zen monastery, we were told that we did not necessarily need time to gain enlightenment, but it would take intention, commitment, and the ability to still our minds and open our hearts.

Are you living your passion? Are you following your dreams? If not, you have eight days to initiate powerful shifts in your life. Reinstate your intention—after all, miracles can happen in eight days. You can do it. Go for it today!

All my love,
Denise

Day 20 (Fire): Your Spiritual Allies

You are a powerful spiritual being, even if you are not consciously aware of it. You have the ability to make a difference in the world through your love, your prayers, your compassion, and your kindness. And the more you give, the more you receive. It is a universal law.

Let this day be filled with the action of kindness.

Affirmation for the Day

"I am a loving spiritual being."

Today

Find as many ways as you can to be a silent emissary of kindness. Do something today to make a difference in the world, or even in one person's world.

Overview

- *Committed to Change!*
  Level 1: Open Your Wings

- *Going for It!*
  Level 2: Soaring on Your Wings of Light

- *Playing Full Out!*
  Level 3: Flying on Wings of Love

Level 1: Open Your Wings

There is an angelic energy within you, which is sweet, pure, and serene, and has always been with you. You have an enormous capacity to love deeply and fully and to pour forth loving energy into the world. However, over the years your wings may have become clipped due to shame, grief, mistreatment, dishonor, fear, or despair. Perhaps your inner light has dimmed.

Today, visualize yourself with shimmering wings of light. Imagine that you are folding these wings around people in need. You might also want to imagine embracing family members, people with whom you have had challenges, or even world situations with your wings. As you go through your day, imagine loving everyone and everything—from the strangers you see on the street to trees and buildings. As you radiate your love and prayers with a purity of heart, you *will* make a difference.

Level 2: Soaring on Your Wings of Light

Fire Week is the time for action. What can you do today that will uplift someone? *Commit a random act of kindness today.* Is there someone you could call who would feel great just hearing from you? Maybe there is a stranger you could inspire or help, or you could pay for the toll of the person behind you. Perhaps you could give a co-worker flowers "just because." It could be as simple as sharing a smile with everyone you meet.

Perhaps you have had a difficult time with an associate. If you can do this in a way that is authentic and true to your soul, today might be a good day to pick out a gift for that person and say, "I saw this and thought of you. I hope you enjoy it."

Write in your Process Journal your acts of kindness today and how you felt during and after you did them.

Level 3: Flying on Wings of Love

It is said that the greatest mystics in history secretly provided great kindness without ever being acknowledged or thanked. The act of compassion was enough— it was not necessary that everyone knew what they did and thanked them for it.

Today, do something that will create a positive impact in the world. It might be something as simple as sending flowers to a new neighbor with a note saying, "Welcome to the neighborhood—I am glad you are here! (From an anonymous future friend.)" Or perhaps you could secretly help a stranger by shoveling their car out of the snow.

The assignment is to do something that empowers, supports, inspires, or contributes to the well-being of one or more people . . . and *never* tell anyone it was you. This kind of giving will make your entire being radiate with incredible light. Today, fly on your wings of love and light!

✿ ✿ ✿

Day 21

Hi!

It is the last day of Fire! You may be happy about this, because although emotions tend to come up in Water Week, often anger, frustration, and irritation come up to be released during Fire Week.

We are moving into Earth tomorrow, which should help ground some of the emotions that have been flowing so freely in the last couple of weeks. But for today, we are still in fire.

I think you will like today, for its focus is on creativity and abundance.

All my love,
Denise

Day 21 (Fire): Fanning the Flame of Your Creativity

Although today's world revolves around goals, accomplishments, and being productive, we each need to have a part of life that is completely free, a place where we can surrender, trust our instincts, and discover and express our soul. The soul needs creativity to express itself. Basically *creativity* is *receptivity*—that is, when you are open and receptive, ideas and inspiration flow. Creativity is one of the easiest ways to hear the messages of the soul.

People often equate creativity with the fine arts (such as painting or writing), but it can also stoke the fires of every area of your life. For example, research has shown that individuals who succeed in business often have a high level of creativity.

To fan the flames of your own creativity, it is essential to be open to all of the ideas that emerge within you, even if they seem wild or unpractical. And for heaven's sake, don't judge these inspired ideas. Nothing dampens creativity faster than thoughts such as "I am not a creative person" or "This is not very good." If you unconditionally accept doubts and negative judgments about your ideas, it will put out your fire.

When you are being truly creative, time stands still, and you enter into a dimension that can carry you beyond the ordinariness of life. Ancient mystics knew this, which is why they often used artistic expression to enter into spiritual trance states.

Affirmation for the Day

"Incredible creative life force flows through my entire being."

Today

Let your creative juices flow today. Find ways in which you can do things differently. Creativity flows when you are out of your routine. Is there a different and creative way that you could set the table, wash the car, or make dinner?

Overview

- *Committed to Change!*
  Level 1: Color Your Feelings

- *Going for It!*
  Level 2: Boundless Creativity

- *Playing Full Out!*
  Level 3: Stoking the Fires of Abundance

Level 1: Color Your Feelings

Get some colored pens, pencils, or crayons and some paper. Close your eyes and notice what you are feeling. What emotional state are you in right now? Now choose a color or colors that represent that feeling and passionately draw the feeling. (I suggest that you play music while you do this exercise, since music often ignites creativity.)

Take out a second sheet of paper, and close your eyes again. This time, be aware of an emotion that you *would like* to feel. Again, choose colors that represent that feeling and draw that emotion. Your drawings do not have to be beautiful, have perspective, or even make sense. You are just opening the doors for your inner wisdom to flow through.

Now close your eyes and ask yourself, "If my soul had something to tell me about today, what would it be?" It is much easier for your soul to speak to you when you have opened the gates, and creativity helps you with this. Draw something that symbolizes the message you get. If you are unsure what the message is, just start drawing or even doodle (often the message will appear in a symbolic form in your doodle).

Level 2: Boundless Creativity

One of the greatest blocks to creativity is the desire to get the approval of others or the need to do it perfectly. Being creative often means defying the norm, or current opinions and beliefs. It means raising your fists to the heavens and declaring, "This is who I am and what I stand for. I don't give a damn about your judgments!" When you do this, you can truly express yourself.

Sometimes creativity also means getting messy and creating projects that are unruly, untidy, and definitely not perfect. Accept that chaos often precedes creativity, so it is not up to you to judge the value of what you have created. The soul of the world needs the rich variety and depth of our creativity in all its forms to stay alive.

For today's exercise, you need three pieces of paper (if possible, get big pieces), pens or crayons, and some music—something that makes you feel good every time you hear it. I suggest that you try different kinds of music while you do this, since different types of music will elicit different aspects of your creativity.

Put the music on, and close your eyes. Ask yourself, "If my soul wanted to tell me something about my spiritual journey in this life, what would it be?" (The soul's message often does not come in words, but in color, shapes, and movement.) Then with your dominant hand (that is, your right hand if you are right-handed), begin to doodle in rhythm to the music as you hold the question in your mind. Be an open, sacred vessel for messages to flow through.

When you are done, take the second piece of paper, but this time do the exercise with your nondominant hand (that is, your left hand if you are right-handed), as you continue to ask your soul what message it has for you.

For the third part of this exercise, doodle and scribble on the third piece of paper with *both* hands. It will be as if your hands are dancing or ice skating with each other. When you are complete, take your drawings and place your hands on them. Close your eyes and ask what message your soul has for you. Write the messages in your Process Journal.

Level 3: Stoking the Fires of Abundance

Abundance is a state of being. Some people have tremendous wealth yet feel poor, while others have very little money yet feel fabulously prosperous. This is because being abundant is an internal experience rather than an external accumulation of goods. For this exercise, use your creativity to begin to program your subconscious in the direction of greater abundance.

Today, create a collage that makes you feel abundant every time you look at it. (I call these kinds of collages "Vision Seed Maps" because you are "seeding" your future with your "vision" for your future.)

Use torn-out pages from magazines, paints, crayons, objects from nature (moss, feathers), or whatever material you desire. The important thing is that when you look at your collage it creates a *feeling* of abundance and prosperity within you. When you feel prosperous, it is much easier to create prosperity. Your collage does not need to be perfect—go quickly and let it flow out of you. Have fun!

Hang your Vision Seed Map in a place where it can impact your subconscious mind and where it becomes a constant subliminal affirmation of the ever-expanding abundance in all areas of your life!

❖ ❖ ❖

CHAPTER FOUR:

Earth Week— Clearing Your Physical Self

Iloved spending time alone in nature when I was a child. When I was five, my family lived in the foot-hills of the Santa Lucia Mountains in California. In those days, I could look as far as my eyes could see and not see a single house—just golden grass-covered hills, ancient gnarled oak trees, and mist-covered mountains in the distance. In the woods near our home, I dug a secret hole in the earth beneath an old oak. I made it deep enough so that I could comfortably curl up in it. I can remember how comforted and safe I felt—snuggled into the earth. It was a haven where I felt nurtured, protected, and embraced.

Earth Week focuses on your physical environment, nurturing yourself and your body, and connecting to the earth itself. All the solid forms around you, including your body, are a part of the physical realm. Ancient peoples understood that everything you see and touch—every stone and every tree, your own body as well as the bodies of all the creatures you encounter—is connected to the body of Mother Earth. This week focuses on your connection and relationship to that physical reality.

The Next Seven Days

Every morning for the next week when you first wake up, focus on the physical nature of your environment. Note the shapes and textures of the objects around you. Get a sense of the solid physical nature of your body. Observe how you relate to and identify with the physical universe.

During Earth Week

- Become more connected to your body.

- Attend to your health.

- Detoxify your body.

- Understand how to use your body's physiology.

- Connect more fully with nature.

- Create a home for your soul.

- Take action for a positive future.

☘ ☘ ☘

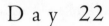

Day 22

Hi!

We are in the final stretch! Today is the first day of Earth. My husband, David, is so glad that Fire Week is over. Without my automatic hot-water kettle, I have almost burned up three pans. I turn on the stove to heat the water for my tea, and then something distracts me, like the phone ringing, and I walk out of the room. David sometimes says that my true Native American name is "Burns Water."

Earth is the time of grounding all the "stuff" that has come up during the last three weeks. It is also the time to gain clarity about what kind of life you desire for yourself and to begin sculpting your body as well as your life.

All my love,
Denise

Day 22 (Earth): Connecting with Your Body

Your physical body is your tool for experiencing the world. It allows you to see, hear, feel, taste, smell, touch, and know your inner and outer environments. It is also the temple for your soul. Your soul is constantly communicating with you through your body, but often you are too busy to really hear these messages. So today begins a journey to begin to hear the messages of your body and soul.

Affirmation for the Day

"I am one with the earth. I am one with my body."

Today

Take a short time to do a meditation / creative visualization in which you imagine that you are Planet Earth. Alternatively, imagine that you have transformed into an aspect of the earth, such as: an old oak tree with your roots sinking deep into the earth; a clean, snowcapped mountain; a wild-flower swaying in the warm spring breeze; or a beach pebble that has been rounded by the gentle rhythm of the sea.

The truth is that you are a part of all these things—you belong to our vast interconnected universe. This meditation helps you reconnect with the physical unity of all things.

<u>Overview</u>

- *Committed to Change!*
  Level 1: Body Assessment

- *Going for It!*
  Level 2: Commitment to Your Body

- *Playing Full Out!*
  Level 3: Talking to Your Body

Level 1: Body Assessment

Your body is the vehicle through which you experience the world around you. You may love it, hate it, ignore it, or be indifferent to it—nevertheless, it colors all of your experiences. It can accelerate or hinder your ability to commune with your soul.

The first step to using your body as a tool for spiritual attunement is to be aware of where you are right now. Answer *yes* or *no* to the following statements:

____ I am comfortable in my body.

____ My body feels good most of the time.

____ My body is an outer representation of my inner state of being. [If not, what aspects of your body do reflect your inner state and what aspects do not?]

____ When I am in physical discomfort, I know that my body is trying to tell me something, and I take time to listen to it.

___ Sometimes I negatively judge my body.

___ I love and cherish my body.

___ I am content with my weight.

___ My weight is within a healthy range for my body and my age.

___ I am satisfied with the muscle tone of my body.

___ I do great things to cherish and honor my body.

___ I have had a complete and thorough physical checkup in the last couple of years.

___ My teeth are in great shape, and I get periodic cleanings and checkups.

___ I floss regularly.

___ I am happy with my hair, nails, and skin.

___ My eyesight is good. [Or, if you wear glasses:] My prescription is appropriate for my eyes.

___ I hear well.

___ My organs (heart, liver, kidneys, pancreas, spleen,
and so forth) are all in excellent health.

___ My cholesterol count is healthy.

___ My blood pressure is in a good range for my age.

___ My digestive system is excellent.

___ I do not smoke.

___ I do not take habit-forming drugs.

____ My sugar intake is appropriate for my body.

____ My alcohol intake is appropriate for my body.

____ I walk or exercise at least three times a week.

____ I take time to breathe fully and deeply.

____ My body handles the stress in my life well.

____ I have no habits that contribute to poor health.

____ I get plenty of sleep to fulfill the needs of my body.

____ My colon health is excellent. (That is, I get a colonoscopy every 10 years after age 50, unless I am at high risk.)

For Women

____ I have had my yearly Pap smear.

____ I am confident with my ability to do a breast exam on myself and I do it on a periodic timetable.

____ I have had my bone density tested at least by age 50 [DEXA scan].

For Men

____ I have had my prostate checked (at age 40 and 45 and every two years after 50), and have had a rectal exam every two years after age 40 (yearly after age 50).

Level 2: Commitment to Your Body

What is a commitment that you can make this week that will empower and enliven your body? Make commitments that you will keep. Do not say, "I will not smoke this week" unless you are really willing to keep this commitment. Make your commitment as if your life depended upon it.

It is better to commit to do a yoga stretch for 30 seconds a day and *keep* your commitment, than to make a commitment that you know you will not keep. Remember to celebrate what you *did* do to empower your body, no matter how big or small it was.

Level 3: Talking to Your Body

Close your eyes and slowly go through each part of your body, starting with your right foot. Give each part of yourself a personality, and imagine talking to that part to see if there is anything that it wants you to know. Complete the meditation by telling each part how much you love and appreciate it.

For example, when I did this exercise, I visualized my right foot as a wise old woman. I asked her if she had anything to tell me. She said, "You go barefoot too much, and as a result, I feel all dried up and cracked. Would you please put moisturizing lotion on and wear shoes more often? And be willing to step forward more in life . . . you are holding back!" I completed the meditation by telling my right foot how thankful I was for the amazing job she was doing for me and how beautiful and strong she was.

Talk to each part of your body, and write down what you discovered in your Process Journal. Remember to include your sex organs, and listen carefully to the messages you receive. Every gland and organ in your body is a precious part of the miracle of life. When we think of our eyes or ears, we do not think of these areas as being shameful, so why should we think about our genitals in such a way? Every part of the body is natural and valuable. It is important to learn to love your body because if you don't, how can you love *yourself?*

At the end of this exercise, go into a meditative state and ask your soul if it has any messages for you. (Taking time to listen to your body creates an opening for the messages of the soul to be heard.)

✿ ✿ ✿

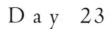

D a y 23

Hi!
Well, we spent three weeks detoxifying our mind, our homes, and our emotions. Now it is time to begin to detox the body! Grab your hats—it is time to go!
All my love,
Denise

Day 23 (Earth): Body Detox

There is a powerful correlation between your mind, your body, your spirit, and your emotions. If your body is sluggish and stagnant, it is easy to feel emotionally stagnant. When your body is vibrant and singing with life-force energy, your spirit soars.

Modern life is often toxic to the soul. In addition to the stress of constantly hurrying and being busy, we also do not always take time to eat in a leisurely way—instead, we grab fast food, chug it down, do not taste it, and run on to the next thing. Much of our water and air is polluted, and much of our food has been produced using pesticides and chemicals. To maintain a healthy environment for the soul, it is valuable to periodically detoxify the body.

Affirmation for the Day

"My mind, body, and spirit are clear channels for Love (or Kindness / God / Goddess / Creator / Universal Life Force)."

Today

Breathe deeply. Drink lots of water. Eat lightly, from fresh food that has a life force. Walk, dance, move your body, and stretch.

Overview

- *Committed to Change!*
  Level 1: Dry Brush Your Skin

- *Going for It!*
  Level 2: Cleanse or Clog

- *Playing Full Out!*
  Level 3: Elimination

Level 1: Dry Brush Your Skin

Dry brushing your skin has been called a miracle technique, for it is a quick, easy, inexpensive, and highly effective way to help detoxify your body. Within a few days, your skin will glow, and your entire body will be stimulated.

Detoxifying by skin brushing does three things to help cleanse your body:

1. It stimulates the lymphatic system, which helps detoxify your body.

2. It sloughs off dead cells so that your skin can breathe. In fact, if your skin were completely engulfed (with paint, for example), after a while your body would start to suffocate. The pores in your skin are absolutely necessary to help oxygenate your body.

3. It allows for a greater release of perspiration because it unclogs pores that are covered with dry skin. (Perspiration has a similar chemical composition to urine; hence, the skin has been called "the third kidney" because it releases the body's waste products.)

Dry brush your skin just before you shower with (optimally) a natural fiber brush. Start at your feet and work your way up, brushing lightly over your neck and face. If you do not have a brush, then a rough towel can be effective. Use brisk, vigorous, rubbing movements, and then shower to slough off all the dead skin. Complete with a brisk, cold rinse.

Level 2: Cleanse or Clog

Every piece of food that you put in your body is either going to cleanse and strengthen your body or is going to clog it. For the rest of this week, be aware of the food that you are eating.

Today, with everything you eat, ask yourself, "Does this cleanse or clog me?" If a predominance of the food you eat is clogging, then consider making a commitment for the rest of this program to only put food in your body that heals and cleanses you.

I do not believe that there is one diet that is right for everyone, because we are all unique; however, there is a place within *you* that knows what foods support and empower your body and what foods clog it. Ask your higher self what the most empowering foods you could eat are, and then make a commitment to eat those foods consciously and conscientiously for the next six days.

Level 3: Elimination

There are lots of ways to detoxify your body. You can eat lighter, cleaner fare, for example, by consuming lots of raw organic vegetables and salads. You can also drink detoxifying herbal teas or "green" drinks. Another way to help cleanse your body is to increase the amount of water you drink, or simply drink your water with a squeeze of fresh lemon. Alternatively, you can cleanse yourself by doing rapid breathing alternating with deep, full breathing. You can also sign up for colonics to cleanse your bowels.

My suggestion is to invest in a series of colonics for deep internal cleansing; however, this method is not available or appropriate for everyone. So for today's exercise, go into a meditative state and ask your higher self what you could do for today (and the next six days) that would be of the greatest value to cleanse and eliminate toxins from your body. Then take steps to follow the wisdom of your soul.

✡ ✡ ✡

Day 24

Hi!

    I continue to be amazed at the synchronicities of the elements. After yesterday's detoxifying, David and I are coincidentally cleaning the mud out of our home and off the walkways. (When we dug up the land for the plumbing, mud and dirt were piled everywhere. So today we are cleansing the walkways outside and the floors inside.) Our mud here is adobe, so we have had to scrub the sidewalks by hand because the adobe is so sticky.

    When I went to the acupuncturist today, she said, "Denise, it is really curious, but your liver seems to be going through a huge detox." Apparently, I am experiencing detoxification of both my body and my environment.

    I have heard from so many others who are undergoing similar kinds of coincidences. I believe that these kinds of experiences are an affirmation of the deep inner work that is occurring for us individually and collectively as we do this program.

    I also believe that what we are doing really does make a difference in the world around us. As we clear away old mental and emotional debris to discover the peace that dwells within us, I believe that we are each making a difference to others and even to the world.

    Only four more days to go!

All my love,

Denise

Day 24 (Earth): Using the Physiology of Your Body

Your physiology (the way you carry yourself and the way you move your body) is one of the most powerful ways that you can impact your life. In other words, if you carry yourself in a way that says, "I am confident, strong, and at peace with myself and the world," your body will send messages to your mind to reconfigure internal processes until they are consistent with your physiology. So if you want to feel confident, adjust your body so that it portrays confidence.

Try this: Hang your head down, frown, slump your shoulders, breathe in a shallow way, and try to feel fabulous and vital without changing your body! Now throw your shoulders back, lift your chin, stand up tall and straight, look up, and put a huge grin on your face. While maintaining that physiology, try to feel depressed. If you keep your body in that peak position, it is almost impossible to feel down in the dumps.

Remember: The way you use your body is the secret key to how you feel.

Affirmation for the Day
"My body is incredibly strong and healthy."

Today

Carry yourself as if an incredible life force and confidence was flowing out of every pore of your body.

Overview

- *Committed to Change!*
  Level I: What Does Your Body Say about You?

- *Going for It!*
  Level 2: Change Your Body, Change Your Life

- *Playing Full Out!*
  Level 3: Rejuvenation Time

Level 1: What Does Your Body Say about You?

It is so easy to read other people through the way they carry themselves. As they grow up, people adopt beliefs about who they are and about their values and rules for life, and each belief has an associated physiology. People who believe that they will always be downtrodden by life will adopt a physiology that says: "I am a downtrodden person." Their bodies become so used to that position that *even when they are not feeling downtrodden* their bodies stay in that position, which will make them feel depressed.

Your body is always communicating statements about who you are to the world. This is great when the message empowers you, but it is not so great if the message does not empower and support you.

If a stranger were to watch the way you use your body, what kind of judgments might that person make about you? Would he or she think that you are tired, arrogant, loving, peaceful, submissive, stressed, confident, shy, kind, busy, overwhelmed, centered, frenetic, honest, dishonest, angry, or joyous? Today, notice how you hold and carry your body. Is it communicating a message that you are satisfied with?

Level 2: Change Your Body, Change Your Life

You can change the way you feel and even dramatically change your life by just changing your physiology. Your emotions are a complex pattern of physiological states that are triggered by the way your body moves and the way you hold yourself. When your brain gets messages from your body that you feel great, then that is what you become. And when your brain gets messages that you are stagnant or afraid or depressed, then *that* is what you become.

Today, choose how you want to feel, and then act as if you are feeling that way. You might decide to feel a quality such as incredible confidence, deep inner peace, ecstatic joy, remarkable courage, infinite wisdom, or whatever your most important value is. Stand in front of a mirror and arrange your facial muscles, the way you stand, your shoulders, the way you breathe, and your entire body into the state you desire. Then continually put yourself into that empowering physiological state.

Walk and move today as if you were totally experiencing the positive quality that you have chosen. This communicates in a dynamic way to your soul that this is who you truly are. It also communicates to others that this is who you are, and they will reflect that back to you.

Level 3: Rejuvenation Time

In addition to periodically carrying your body in ways that exemplify a quality such as vitality, confidence, or grace, it is also immensely valuable to take time to use your body's physiology to exemplify rest, relaxation, and rejuvenation.

It is so easy to get caught up in the hectic pace of life and forget the importance of rest and rejuvenation. We forget how necessary it is to take time throughout each day to renew and recover our life forces. We often give out so much energy all day that it is difficult to completely recoup and recover that energy during the night, so we are often in an energy-deficient state without a reserve to call upon.

To build an enormous reserve of energy, it is essential to periodically take time to rejuvenate yourself, and you can use your physiology to do this. For example, when you are truly relaxed and at peace, how do you hold your body? Are your shoulders relaxed? Is your breath slow and deep? Are the muscles in your face soft and relaxed? Are you softly smiling? Today, every couple of hours, take seven to ten minutes to recharge by changing your physiology into a state of peace, serenity, softness, receptivity, and joy. By doing so, you will begin to develop a bountiful reserve of life force.

Day 25

Hi!

Well, I have made it so far in Earth with no major mishap. David has been worried that we would have an earthquake or something after all the excitement in Water and Fire. But so far, so good. We have put in lots of plants and now have 30 fruit trees in the ground (they all look like sticks right now, but someday they will be pregnant with fruit).

We have also bought bags of seeds at the farm supply store that are going to be planted in the next couple of days. There is something so satisfying about putting a tiny object into the earth and watching it become a glorious plant, resplendent with flowers or fruit, a few months later.

This 28-day sojourn has been such a remarkable experience for me. It is difficult to believe that we only have three more days after this. But I believe in "going for it" to the end, so I am gearing up. (Keep in mind that there is one last thing to do after the program is complete. But I will let you know more about that later.)

All my love,
Denise

Day 25 (Earth): Awakening the Natural Forces Within You

We live in a rhythmic universe—every part of nature has a unique language and rhythm of its own . . . every flower, bird, and tree has its own language, which together create the underlying context that weaves all life together. We are constantly surrounded by these rhythms of energy. And if we take a moment to become very still, we can feel these rhythms of the natural world inside of us.

Affirmation for the Day

"I am in harmony with the natural rhythm of life."

Today

Be aware of the rhythms of nature in all its forms around you—from the rising and setting sun, to the lengthening of shadows during the day, to the movement of animals and insects, and the changing weather patterns. Also, tune in to your own internal rhythms—do they seem to be in alignment with nature's rhythms?

<u>Overview</u>

- *Committed to Change!*
  Level 1: Replenished by Nature

- *Going for It!*
  Level 2: Become the Earth

- *Playing Full Out!*
  Level 3: Awakening Natural Rhythms Within You

Level 1: Replenished by Nature

As nature is disappearing around us, we are losing vast tracts of the wilderness inside of ourselves as well. It is as if the fertile soil of the soul is being gradually depleted. Every day, as we lose part of our natural outer heritage, our inner heritage diminishes as well.

One of the fastest ways to replenish the reserves of the soul is to spend time in nature. The remarkable thing about the human brain is that research has shown that even just visualizing nature can produce some of the same positive biochemical and psychological results as actually spending time in it.

Today, take 15 minutes to close your eyes and imagine yourself in a beautiful, refreshing place in nature. Make it as real as you can, and imagine yourself really being there. You might visualize a mountain meadow, a sunny seashore, an alpine lake surrounded by snowcapped mountains, or somewhere else. (This is an excellent exercise to do periodically during the day, as even a few seconds of visualizing yourself in nature can rejuvenate you.)

Level 2: Become the Earth

Native peoples understood that the earth is alive and all of nature is interconnected. They knew that every human is a part of nature, not separate from it. To activate hidden forces within yourself, one of the most powerful exercises that you can do is to imagine yourself as the earth and/or various aspects of the earth. To do this, enter into a meditative space.

Imagine that your body is beginning to expand until you feel yourself as the earth. Feel the deep heat in your core. Be aware of the great mountains and deep oceans upon your surface. Feel yourself revolving around the powerful force of the sun. Half of you is in the sunlight, while the other half is in the dark. You are always a balance of dark and light. And you are spinning in a vast and infinite cosmos.

At the completion of this exercise, you might also want to imagine yourself as various aspects of the earth. For example, imagine becoming an oak tree, a golden hill, a craggy mountain, or a blade of grass. Some traditions use the word *shape-shifting* to describe the ability to enter into the consciousness of various aspects of nature. Imagine that you are shape-shifting or dissolving into the consciousness of the aspect of nature that you have chosen. Write in your Process Journal what it felt like to be, for example, a seashore pebble, a willow tree, or a rose.

Level 3: Awakening Natural Rhythms Within You

Go out into nature at some point today. It does not have to be a national park or wilderness area—it can be your backyard or a neighborhood park. Lean up against a tree, lay on the earth, sink your toes into the sand, or put your palms on the moss. Really let your body experience a tactile connection to nature. Even if there is snow on the ground, go outside and scoop up a handful, smell it, let a bit of it melt on your tongue, and touch it to your face. Or if you are in an urban apartment and cannot possibly find any nature, then open a window and inhale the wind and look at the clouds or the stars. Embrace the forces of nature around you with your body in some way today.

Once you have a tactile connection with nature, close your eyes and feel yourself dissolving into the ground. Feel the sweet soul of the earth merge with your soul.

As you become very still doing this exercise, you can begin to sense how the rhythms of the natural world are merging and interwoven with your own internal rhythms. Write about the experience you had doing this exercise in your Process Journal.

✤ ✤ ✤

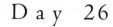

Day 26

Hi!

This morning we had an amazing downpour. As lightning crackled and thunder roared, the rain pounded the house so hard that water flooded under the front door, which is up two steps. Yet after the deluge, a huge rainbow rippled across the sky, and the moist earth smelled so good.

Today's assignment is about something close to my heart—creating a home for the soul. I hope you enjoy this day.

All my love,

Denise

Day 26 (Earth): A Home for the Soul

I believe that there are four things that the soul requires in a home: First, it needs a sense of belonging, to feel connected to the land or a place; second, it needs a place to feel safe, so you can be yourself without fear or hesitation; third, it yearns for harmony with the greater cycles of nature; and finally, your soul needs sacred space.

When your home has these things, your life will be filled with inner peace.

AFFIRMATION FOR THE DAY

"I am at home, no matter where I am."

Today

Wherever you are, affirm that you are "at home." For example, if you are in your car, affirm: "I am at home in my car." If you are in your office, say: "I am at home in my office." If you are on a bus, repeat: "I am at home on the bus."

If you are with other people, affirm: "I am at home with [Sue and John, or my children, or my husband or my wife, and so on]." Also, periodically affirm: "I am at home in my body."

Overview

- *Committed to Change!*
  Level 1: Bring Nature into Your Home

- *Going for It!*
  Level 2: Create a Place in Your Home for Your Soul

- *Playing Full Out!*
  Level 3: Creating Sacred Space

Level 1: Bring Nature into Your Home

The survival of the earliest humans depended on their ability to live in balance with the natural world, and their homes reflected an awareness of this fact. Unfortunately, modern homes are often separated from nature, and the soul has suffered as a result.

Today, bring nature into your environment so that the "beauty in your home leads the heart to the holy mountain." Find a way to implement the *feeling* of nature by bringing it into your home. Here are some ideas:

- Put up a photo of nature.

- Create an arrangement of leaves, moss, pinecones, and stones on a table.

- Tie feathers on strings and let them dangle where a breeze can softly move them.

- Put a big plant by the front door.

- Take a walk, find some items from nature, and arrange them into a mandala on a coffee table.

- Play CDs of nature sounds, such as a waterfall, raindrops, the ocean surf, wind, crickets, birds, and so on.

Level 2: Create a Place in Your Home for Your Soul

Imagine that you are hand in hand with your soul, walking through your home. What places nourish and comfort your soul? What places do not? Go through each room and ask your soul if there is a way that the space could be even more conducive to its well-being.

When you are complete with this exercise, begin to take action. For example, if your soul says, "This room feels great, but it would be nice to have some fresh flowers," bring home a pretty bouquet to enhance the energy of that room.

Locate one place in your home that will be your power spot, and make sure that it is clear and clean. In that space, put objects that inspire you and are beautiful or meaningful, such as favorite photos, crystals, flowers, candles, or special stones. This place does not have to be large, but it should be big enough for you to use for meditation or relaxation, or where you can simply sit and rejuvenate your spirit. For example, it could be a comfortable chair by a sunny window where you sit to replenish your energy.

Level 3: Creating Sacred Space

It is valuable to have at least one place in the home that honors the sacred aspects of life—an altar is one way of accomplishing this. A home altar is like a small temple in your house, which can assist you on your journey toward healing and integration and can serve as a reminder of the sacred aspects of life.

Many people today think that altars are religious and only of significance inside a church; however, for thousands of years, people created altars in their dwellings. These sanctified areas were spiritual and provided a sacred space, a visible symbol of the connection between heaven and earth. Altars were a reminder of the mysteries of the universe and served as a focal point for communing with spiritual realms.

Create an altar today dedicated to your soul and the souls of those who share your space. On it put reminders of what feeds your soul. For example, you might place seashells there that you found at the beach during your vacation because they remind you of those joyous moments by the sea. You might also include a feather as a reminder to take life lightly. Another idea is to place photos of family members and loved ones on your altar.

After gathering the objects, place each object on your altar with a sense of grace. Speak aloud from your heart about the deeper, underlying meaning of each object. Complete your altar with a blessing for your home. (As a suggestion, you may want to have objects that represent Air, Water, Fire, and Earth as well as the Creator on your altar to serve as subliminal reminders of the natural and spiritual worlds.)

Day 27

Hi!

It is so beautiful this morning: A thick fog has settled in the valley; and the pine trees and gnarled oak trees, which are darkly silhouetted against the white mists, look like stoic, mystical guardians.

I have been so blessed these last few days to have a visit from my friends Pattie and Linda, who are here helping me open boxes and sort through things. Pattie is the Clutter-Clearing Queen—for years, she lived with less than you could fit into a suitcase. And Linda is the Queen of Labeling.

Although David and I have lived in this house for two years, everything has been in storage during the remodeling and construction. It seems to be a remarkable coincidence that I am finally going through my stuff during the 28-day clearing program.

It has been so funny to watch myself during this process. Although I know the importance of clutter-clearing, I am experiencing attachment and fear as I am opening boxes. At one point, when I saw an old strainer in the trash, I lamented, "Someone threw away my strainer without asking!"

Patti logically said, "Denise, that strainer has a hole in it, and you have another one that is in perfect condition."

Meekly I replied, "Well, I might need it to sift sand someday."

She benignly smiled and handed me the strainer. A couple hours later, when no one was watching, I threw it away.

Last night I lay in bed listening to peals of laughter rocketing off the walls. This morning Linda and Pattie (the sources of the laughter) said, "Open the linen closet." When

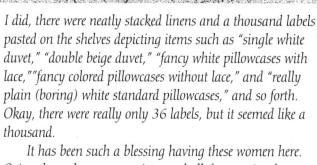

I did, there were neatly stacked linens and a thousand labels pasted on the shelves depicting items such as "single white duvet," "double beige duvet," "fancy white pillowcases with lace,""fancy colored pillowcases without lace," and "really plain (boring) white standard pillowcases," and so forth. Okay, there were really only 36 labels, but it seemed like a thousand.

It has been such a blessing having these women here. Going through my possessions and all the associated emotions made me even more aware of how challenging our clutter can be. We really do reveal ourselves in our stuff.

Today's assignment is focused on sending your intention and energy into the future. I love doing these exercises. I hope you will, too.

All my love,
Denise

Day 27 (Earth): Creating a Fabulous Future

You have spent time during this program clearing your mental, emotional, physical, and spiritual clutter to make it easier to hear the messages from your soul. Today you have the opportunity to begin to manifest a future that will *nourish* your soul.

Affirmation for the Day

"My future is filled with love, joy, and peace!"

Today

Act today in accordance with whom you desire to be tomorrow. Tomorrow's future is being created today, and today is yesterday's future.

In other words, your future is created now. If whom you desire to be in the future is strong, beautiful, and fit, act as if you are these qualities now. Do not slump your shoulders and drag your feet—stand tall, square your head on your shoulders, and walk with confidence and deliberation. As you feel it, so you become it. This is a simple yet powerful truth.

Overview

- *Committed to Change!*
  Level 1: Creating Your Future

- *Going for It!*
  Level 2: Project Yourself into Your Future

- *Playing Full Out!*
  Level 3: Taking Action for a Positive Future

Level 1: Creating Your Future

Close your eyes and spend 15 minutes visualizing an amazing future. Make it almost like an epic movie.

For example, David and I recently planted our first vines for our vineyard, so for this exercise, I might imagine myself six years in the future. . . . The sun is setting and frogs are beginning to croak, and a huge moon is rising in the east. I am with a group of good friends in our new home on the hill, and we are all toasting each other because our vineyard's wine tastes so good. I put some music on, and we all spontaneously start dancing through the wild grasses as the moon rises.

Imagine yourself in the future doing something that would nourish your soul. Immerse yourself so much in the experience that it feels real. By doing so, you are projecting the energy into the future so it can draw to it the forces it needs to manifest. Affirm to yourself that this, or something better for your highest good, will come to fruition.

Level 2: Project Yourself into Your Future

Take some time to design your future. Write it down as if you were composing from the vantage point of one year in the future. Write in a very loving and kind way, and congratulate yourself for all that you have experienced and whom you have become. For example, you might write: "The last year has been amazing! I finished writing my book and found a great publisher. I am so

glad. I also focused on my health in this last year, finally joining a gym that I attended on a consistent basis. I am so proud of myself! Plus, my body is stronger than it has been in years." Then, do this exercise from the vantage points of 3, 5, 10, 15, and 20 years in the future.

Level 3: Taking Action for a Positive Future

There is a direct correlation between your thoughts and emotions and what you create for yourself in the future. For example, the more confident you currently feel, the more likely you are to have a confident future. And the more you feel afraid, the more you are likely to have a fearful future.

Today's assignment may be a bit challenging, but it is well worth the rewards. From the moment you read this assignment—I mean from *right now* until you go to bed tonight—act as if your compelling future has already happened.

For example, if your desire for the future is to feel deep inner peace, then act as if you already have it. Walk as if you already have inner peace. Move your facial muscles in the same way that someone who has inner peace would. Carry yourself as if you have deep serenity, and even dress as if you have inner peace. Think in the way someone who has inner peace would think. Every time you catch yourself acting in any other way, snap yourself back into the positive persona of your future self.

The future is being created right now. So right now, this minute, begin to create the positive future you desire. Instead of "I will believe it when I see it," your motto is, "I will see it when I believe it." Begin believing right now that you can and will have an incredible future, no matter how unlikely it may seem from where you are in your life circumstances. And so it will be!

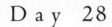

Day 28

Hi!

You did it! Today is the last day of the 28-day program. Although I am a bit sad for this to end, as it has been an exquisite journey, I am exhilarated by the next step.

I hope you enjoy this last day of the program. It has been an honor to share it with you. Thank you for being in my life. I look forward to when we meet again.

All my love,
Denise

Day 28 (Earth): A Circle of Love

At its essence, the soul is unconditional love. When you have cleared away inner and outer clutter, your capacity to love yourself, love others, and love the Creator magnifies. Today is a reminder of who you are.

Affirmation for the Day

"I give love deeply and fully. I receive love deeply and fully. My essence is love."

Today

Continually remind yourself that no matter what judgments you make, every experience you have is allowing you to evolve as a spiritual being. Remind yourself that everything today is for your ultimate <u>highest</u> good, even if you judge it as a bad, boring, demeaning, or worthless experience.

Overview

- *Committed to Change!*
  Level 1: Surrounded by a Circle of Love

- *Going for It!*
  Level 2: Opening Your Heart of Light

- *Playing Full Out!*
  Level 3: Go to the Center of Your Being

Level 1: Surrounded by a Circle of Love

Meditate on the sky. Visualize a sparkling spring morning with no clouds. The sky is completely clear—breathe in this clarity. Absorb the vastness into your soul. Become one with the sky.

Then imagine yourself in a beautiful fresh mountain meadow. As you stand in the center of an ancient and sacred circle of stones, you find yourself surrounded by a circle of love. All around you are people who love you, angelic beings, and wise ones from the realm of spirit. They are radiating incredible love and healing energy to you.

Level 2: Opening Your Heart of Light

No matter where you are or what you do today—whether you are walking, eating, working, talking, standing, or sitting—remind yourself that at your core, you are love and light. Physicists now agree with what ancient mystics have always known: that your physical body is composed of vast space. From a spiritual perspective, within this vastness dwells light, *your* light, which can be accessed by meditation.

Visualize a small sun or a burning flame shimmering in the center of your chest. Then imagine this light radiating out through your body until your entire being is engulfed in it. There is now an orb of light around you.

Whenever you encounter anyone, visualize your light radiating from your heart to his or her heart. Wherever you go today, let your radiance flow out of you to animals, people, plants, trees, environments, homes, and everything. Do not tell anyone what you are doing.

Allow your light to infuse a warmth to everyone and everything around you. If you continue this practice past today, your inner flame will grow in brilliance and warmth. Others will feel embraced by your presence and will be healed by your warmth.

Level 3: Go to the Center of Your Being

To go to the center of your being, you need to let go of your mind, your thoughts, and your ideas. You need to let go of preconceived notions about what your soul is and spiral into the sweetness of your being.

One way to do this is to *shake!* Put some rhythmic music on. Wear loose clothing, breathe fully and deeply, and begin to shake. Let your body vibrate, and lose your mind. Allow every cell in you to respond to the music.

The shaking is wonderful because it gets you out of your normal body postures that define and confine you. Shake! Be wild! Dissolve yourself and your identity. If you get tired, keep shaking. Go through the tiredness to the other side where you feel your shaking as a kind of flow.

Then collapse. Turn off the music, close your eyes, and softly travel to the inner sacred place within you where the resting place of your soul dwells. Be aware of emotions, feelings, images, and symbols that appear. And be aware if *nothing* appears. This is also a message from your soul—it is a message of the beauty and the holiness of nothingness and stillness.

CHAPTER FIVE:

Quest—Beyond
the 28 Days

∞

You have spent 28 days examining your life, clearing your closets, and opening your heart in order to hear the messages from your soul. One of the best ways to open to your higher self and your inner wisdom is to take time away from your routine to be very still and just listen. This is a kind of quest, and it would be best to do it in the next two weeks. You can spend an hour, several hours, half a day, or even an entire day dedicated to praying and listening.

For this type of quest, you might want to make a sacred circle to sit in. To make this circle, use objects to represent Air, Water, Fire, and Earth for the four cardinal directions. For example, you might put a feather in the eastern part of the circle to represent Air, a bowl of water in the southern part of the circle to represent Water, a candle in the west for Fire, and a crystal or stone in the north for Earth.

You can make your sacred circle inside or outdoors in nature. It can be a small circle four to six feet across, or a larger circle that is eight to ten feet across. You can make your circle from flowers, pebbles, pinecones, or anything that you have available. The objects you use are less important than the feeling that you have within your circle. It is essential that when you are sitting in your circle, you feel safe, and it becomes your sanctuary.

Once your circle is complete, create a ceremony to sanctify and bless it, and ask for spiritual guidance. Then sit in your circle and visualize yourself becoming a sacred vessel for spirit to flow through. Pray. Talk to the Creator. Be still. Breathe. Be open. You might want to have pen and paper to record any insights that you have.

Watch for signs. There will be messages all around you. If you are outdoors, watch the movement of the animals, birds, and clouds. If you are indoors, try to be in a place where you can see out of a window. Notice the movements of the clouds or what occurs outside, but also be aware of signs within your home. For example, if you are sitting in your home in your sacred circle and a trail of ants begins to weave its way toward you, this might be a message for you about "working in community."

Often your soul will speak to you in symbols, and during your quest you may receive signs that are messages from your soul. . . .

- Listen.

- If you knew what your soul wanted you to know, what would it be?

- Watch your thoughts and feelings and the events around you. Listen with your heart.

- When you are complete with the listening phase, then send prayers and blessings to your friends and family.

- Pray for people you knew in the past, and for those you have wronged or who have wronged you.

- Pray for people you barely know or people you do not know now, but will know in the future.

- Pray for world leaders and tense global situations.

- Pray intensely. Pray sweetly and softly for yourself and those you love. Dissolve your entire being into the prayer. Let go! Pray like you have never prayed before.

- When you are complete, disassemble your circle and give thanks for all the blessings that you have received.

In powerful and often mysterious ways, the effects of this program will manifest in your life for years to come.

✾ ✾ ✾

You have my love and support on your continuing journey to the soul,
— Denise

About the Author

Denise Linn is an international healer, writer, and lecturer. She has taught seminars in 19 countries and has written 17 books, including the best-selling book *Sacred Space* and the award-winning books *Sacred Legacies* and *Secrets & Mysteries.* She has also appeared on *The Oprah Winfrey Show* and in numerous documentaries, as well as on TV programs on the Discovery and Lifetime Networks and BBC television.

Denise lives in the central California wine region, where she and her husband, David, have a small vineyard and winery ("Sacred Oak") dedicated to producing sacred wine. Denise also currently leads professional certification courses in Soul Coaching.

Website: **www.DeniseLinn.com**

✿ ✿ ✿

Denise Linn gives seminars throughout the world. To receive information about her courses, learn how to enroll in her Soul Coaching classes, or get on line support while doing the program, write:

Denise Linn Seminars
P.O. Box 759
Paso Robles, CA 93447-0759

Or visit **www.DeniseLinn.com** or **www.Soul-Coaching.com**

✿ ✿ ✿

Denise's guided meditation tapes, CDs, and videos are available worldwide from:

QED Recording Services Ltd.
Lancaster Road
New Barnet, Herts
EN4 8AS
United Kingdom
Phone: 44-(0)20-8441-7722
E-mail: **enquiry@qed-productions.com**
Website: **www.qed-productions.com**

✿

Hay House Titles of Related Interest

Books

A Deep Breath of Life, by Alan Cohen

Eliminating Stress, Finding Inner Peace (book with CD), by Brian L. Weiss, M.D.

GROW—The Modern Woman's Handbook, by Lynne Franks

Healing with the Angels, by Doreen Virtue

Inner Peace for Busy People, by Joan Z. Borysenko, Ph.D.

The Power of Intention, by Dr. Wayne W. Dyer

Sacred Ceremony, by Steven D. Farmer, Ph.D.

Turning Inward, Cheryl Richardson

Card Decks

Healing Cards, by Caroline Myss and Peter Occhiogrosso

Healing the Mind and Spirit Cards, by Brian L. Weiss, M.D.

I Can Do It® Cards, by Louise Hay

Juicy Living Cards, by SARK

The Mastery of Love Cards, by don Miguel Ruiz

Messages from Your Angels Cards, by Doreen Virtue

Organizing from the Inside Out Cards, by Julie Morgenstern

Self-Care Cards, by Cheryl Richardson

MEDITATE.
VISUALIZE.
LEARN.

Get the **Empower You**
Unlimited Audio *Mobile App*

Get unlimited access to the entire Hay House audio library!

You'll get:

- 500+ inspiring and life-changing **audiobooks**
- 200+ ad-free **guided meditations** for sleep, healing, relaxation, spiritual connection, and more
- Hundreds of audios **under 20 minutes** to easily fit into your day
- **Exclusive content** *only* for subscribers
- No credits, **no limits**

New audios added every week!

★★★★★ **I ADORE this app.** I use it almost every day. Such a blessing. – Aya Lucy Rose

Scan me with your phone camera!

HAY HOUSE

TRY FOR FREE!
Go to: hayhouse.com/listen-free

We hope you enjoyed this Hay House book. If you'd like to receive our online catalog featuring additional information on Hay House books and products, or if you'd like to find out more about the Hay Foundation, please contact:

Hay House, Inc., P.O. Box 5100, Carlsbad, CA 92018-5100
(760) 431-7695 or (800) 654-5126
(760) 431-6948 (fax) or (800) 650-5115 (fax)
www.hayhouse.com® • www.hayfoundation.org

———

Published in Australia by: Hay House Australia Pty. Ltd.,
18/36 Ralph St., Alexandria NSW 2015
Phone: 612-9669-4299 • *Fax:* 612-9669-4144
www.hayhouse.com.au

Published in the United Kingdom by: Hay House UK, Ltd.,
The Sixth Floor, Watson House, 54 Baker Street, London W1U 7BU
Phone: +44 (0)20 3927 7290 • *Fax:* +44 (0)20 3927 7291
www.hayhouse.co.uk

Published in India by: Hay House Publishers India,
Muskaan Complex, Plot No. 3, B-2, Vasant Kunj, New Delhi 110 070
Phone: 91-11-4176-1620 • *Fax:* 91-11-4176-1630
www.hayhouse.co.in

———

Access New Knowledge.
Anytime. Anywhere.

Learn and evolve at your own pace
with the world's leading experts.

www.hayhouseU.com

Free e-newsletters from Hay House, the Ultimate Resource for Inspiration

Be the first to know about Hay House's free downloads, special offers, giveaways, contests, and more!

Get exclusive excerpts from our latest releases and videos from *Hay House Present Moments*.

Our *Digital Products Newsletter* is the perfect way to stay up-to-date on our latest discounted eBooks, featured mobile apps, and Live Online and On Demand events.

Learn with real benefits! *HayHouseU.com* is your source for the most innovative online courses from the world's leading personal growth experts. Be the first to know about new online courses and to receive exclusive discounts.

Enjoy uplifting personal stories, how-to articles, and healing advice, along with videos and empowering quotes, within *Heal Your Life*.

Sign Up Now!

Get inspired, educate yourself, get a complimentary gift, and share the wisdom!

Visit www.hayhouse.com/newsletters to sign up today!